BRITISH AUTO LEGENDS

Michel Zumbrunn

Text by Richard Heseltine

BRITISH AUTO LEGENDS

Classics of Style and Design

MERRELL

LONDON · NEW YORK

First published 2007 by Merrell Publishers Limited

Head office
81 Southwark Street
London SE1 0HX

New York office
740 Broadway, 12th Floor
New York, NY 10003

merrellpublishers.com

British Library Cataloguing-in-Publication Data:
Zumbrunn, Michel
British auto legends : classics of style and design
1. Automobiles – Great Britain – History
I. Title II. Heseltine, Richard
629.2′22′0941

ISBN-13: 978-1-8589-4412-8
ISBN-10: 1-8589-4412-0

Produced by Merrell Publishers Limited
Design concept by Matt Hervey
Layout by Jade Design
Copy-edited by Caroline Ball
Proof-read by Barbara Roby
Indexed by Hilary Bird

Printed and bound in China

Jacket, front: Aston Martin DB4GT Zagato, see p. 177
Jacket, back: Jaguar C-type, see p. 121
Page 2: Jaguar XJ Spider Pininfarina, see p. 249
Page 6: Jaguar C-type, as above
Pages 28–29: Jaguar XK180, see p. 271
Pages 276–77: Jaguar XJ Spider Pininfarina, as above

Acknowledgements

I should like to offer my sincere thanks to all the collectors
of British cars, who, through their collections, are helping
to preserve an important part of British culture. I must
also extend particular thanks to Lukas Hüni, Dr Christian
Jenny and Georges Weidmann.

Michel Zumbrunn

I should like to thank Dave Richards of *Classic &
Sports Car* for sharing his technical knowledge, and
also Gordon Cruickshank of *Motor Sport* for his
amazing powers of recall. This book would not have
been possible without the help of Robert Hui, Chris
Rees and Marion Moisy.

Richard Heseltine

INTRODUCTION

History is written by the victors, so it is said. Not so in the case of the British motor industry, for the simple reason that there no longer is one, at least not anything rooted entirely in the Sceptred Isle. As the global village coalesces, Great Britain's independent players have long since been amalgamated with former rivals, swallowed whole by multinational industrial juggernauts or left to wither and die, no longer able to rely on the succour of state shelter. All this should have left a dent in national pride. The thing is (and this is the important bit), British cars remain among the most highly coveted in the world. Regardless of the nationality of a specific parent company, such names as Aston Martin, Rolls-Royce, Bentley, Jaguar, MG and Lotus – the good stuff – continue to resonate with enthusiasts everywhere. They have heritage, they have breeding and they're really rather good.

The history of the British motor industry is a tale of faltering early steps, appreciation of the automobile, rapid growth, global domination and a slow, often painful decline amid social turmoil and catastrophic complacency. Sprinkled liberally among all this are stories of tremendous human endeavour, of boundary-pushing innovation, throat-catching artistry and universal supremacy in motor sport. For a country of such small size, geographically speaking, Great Britain's role in shaping the history of the automobile cannot be overestimated. This is, after all, the realm that was once responsible for a quarter of the world's automobile production and half of all vehicle exports; the nation that invented and exploited the concept of niche vehicles, most recognizably the sports car; and the manufacturing powerhouse that helped establish overseas marques – the same marques that would, ironically, ultimately lay waste to the home market decades later. It's a compelling and often tortuous saga, and one that's still unravelling.

The introduction of the motor car to Great Britain was slow, as was the gestation of the automobile industry itself. Since the seventeenth century inventive men had wrestled with the challenge of finding a means of motive power as a substitute for horses. Nicolas-Joseph Cugnot, Richard Trevithick, Léon Serpollet, Comte Jules-Albert de Dion (or rather his engineers) and others all

The glorious C-type established Jaguar as a powerhouse in international motor sport, winning the Le Mans 24 Hour endurance classic first time out in 1951. A true British auto legend, it is just one reminder of the nation's peerless automotive endeavours.

The Daimler company is almost as old as the motor car itself, and was Britain's first volume manufacturer, although its roots were grounded firmly in German technological advancement. Above are two Daimler cars, made some hundred years apart.

constructed steam-powered vehicles with varying degrees of success. Further attempts at what nominally passed for internal-combustion engines first appeared as far back as 1805, although the vehicle devised by Swiss designer François Isaac de Rivaz could barely get out of its own way. Belgian-born Frenchman Jean-Joseph Etienne Lenoir's 'car' of 1863 took three hours to cover 6 miles (less than 10 kilometres).

The first truly capable application of engine to vehicle occurred twenty-two years later, when Germany's Karl Benz and then Gottlieb Daimler ushered in the motor car driven by internal combustion. It would be a further nine years before Great Britain caught up, or at least came close, when Frederick Bremer's eponymous creation rolled out of his workshop in Walthamstow, East London, in 1894. The Bremer may have marked Britain's first, hesitant step into automobile legend, but this plumber from London's East End viewed it more as a personal project and, once the car was completed, he turned his attention to other ventures.

The first British Motor Show was held at the Agricultural Halls in London the following year, in 1895, yet the first production car – 'production' being a relative term – didn't arrive until 1896.

And it is to Germany and Gottlieb Daimler that the British motor industry owes its origins, for the Schorndorf-born inventor lent his name to Britain's oldest established car manufacturer. A meeting in 1888 between Herr Daimler and forward-thinking businessman Frederick Richard Simms led to Simms acquiring the licence, three years on, to sell Daimler engines in Great Britain. In 1893 he changed his company's name from F.R. Simms & Co. to Daimler Motor Syndicate, manufacturing engines that were primarily used in water-borne craft. Shortly thereafter a gifted promoter and industrialist, Harry John Lawson, established Daimler as a car manufacturer, after he had bought out Simms to the tune of £150,000. In April 1897 the first Daimler automobile reached its expectant owner, the prototype having been completed twelve months earlier. Lawson, often cited as 'the father of the British motor industry', continued to buy up all manner of motor-related patents while fending off accusations of crooked accounting and double-dealing. In 1904 he was sentenced to twelve months' hard labour in a fraud case (not related to Daimler). This wouldn't be the last time that car manufacture attracted the unscrupulous: conmen and chancers outwitting the easily fleeced was to become a common theme in automobile lore.

The motor car was soon adopted by the affluent and the daring, but it was initially declared antisocial and a hazard to human life: speeds in excess of 20 mph (32 km/h), some said, would result in heads being severed by the sheer force of the rushing air. This was swiftly, and obviously, disproved. Not that it really mattered, as early motorized-vehicle development in Great Britain was severely hindered by archaic laws introduced during the nineteenth century. The Red Flag Act restricted the use of all mechanically propelled vehicles being driven on the public highway. Regulations called for each automobile to have two occupants and for a third person to walk before it waving a red flag. Top speed was restricted to 2 mph (3 km/h) in town and a heady 4 mph (6.5 km/h) in rural areas. The poor unfortunate who had to advance ahead faced injury as impatient drivers in the embryonic stages of road rage could not, or would not, remain at walking pace.

It was only after intense lobbying by enthusiastic owners – and by Lawson, who had many influential friends – that the most severe restrictions were repealed with the Locomotives on Highways Act of 1896. To celebrate this newly won freedom, Lawson organized the first London to Brighton Run (also known as the Emancipation Run) that same year, and the participating motor cars were given starting orders by the symbolic tearing-up of a red flag by the Earl of Winchilsea. Ironically, some participants in the maiden event weren't over-keen to be at one with their machines and instead loaded them on to trains shortly after the start and then appeared suitably weatherbeaten and muddied when they arrived at Madeira Drive, Brighton.

For all the jubilation at emancipation from the Red Flag Act, these early motor cars certainly brought danger, but not from their speed. There was no set template for what an automobile should look like, no cut-and-paste plan to follow, so boffins laboured on all manner of ingenious – and often downright terrifying – ideas. Most of the first cars really did resemble 'horseless carriages', employing the same basic methods of construction in wood and fabric that had existed for centuries, but they experimented with elliptical wheel patterns, two wheels with stabilizers, passengers arranged in *front* of the driver … What they sought was not only speed but also vehicles tough and durable enough to withstand punishment on pre-tarmacadam roads. And without an outline to crib, it was a case of 'if it runs, it's done'. Only lack of imagination blunted designers' sense of daring. Motor cars sparked the inventiveness of creative types and, while many prototypes went unheralded or didn't even reach completion, this sense of capturing the zeitgeist wasn't the mere fad that some predicted. The motor car was here to stay. And how.

ANTIPATHY SUBSIDES AS GREAT BRITAIN ADOPTS THE MOTOR CAR

Demand for automobiles grew steadily during the latter half of the 1890s, with the Benz becoming the global favourite: by 1899 some 2000 had been delivered. Yet motoring was still primarily viewed as a pastime, a distraction for the moneyed, rather than a viable means of mass transport. Few people had even seen a car.

Then, in 1900, the newly formed Automobile Club of Great Britain saw to it that Everyman got a closer look at the motor car by holding its 1000 Miles Trial, which took in most of the key cities of England and Scotland. Predictably, H.J. Lawson was heavily involved, using the event to promote his Daimler and HMC brands; the vast majority of the sixty-five entrants came under his jurisdiction. The participants set off from London's Hyde Park Corner in April of that year, and most of them completed the distance without mishaps. The race went a long way to demonstrating that the motor car was a reliable (all things being relative) means of transport – one that would ultimately change the face of society.

The emergence of what could realistically pass for a British motor industry was slow to take off, however, and was very much dependent on importation of information and technology. The sort of person attracted to this nascent trade, as personified by H.J. Lawson, tended not to be steeped in engineering but was more commonly a speculator. Big business simply wasn't interested, and it was left to the dreamers, schemers, plotters and hucksters to make a go of it. This is in part explained by the higher rate of return on capital investment in other fields. Why should the large engineering businesses that possessed the means and resources to build cars in volume bother with automobiles, when making armaments or ships resulted in greater revenue?

With the exception of such entrepreneurial engineers as Herbert Austin, most of the early British would-be motor moguls never stood a chance because they didn't understand how businesses work. Those who had sufficient backing in place actually to build cars generally tended to put greater emphasis on technical matters than on whether or not there was an end profit to be made. It was this lack of commercial acumen that laid many open to the attentions of the dishonest. An extraordinary 221 firms entered the industry between 1901 and 1905. There were a number of successful company flotations and rather more unsuccessful ones, but by 1914 around 90 per cent of these businesses had either ceased trading or moved away from making automobiles.

This situation wasn't due entirely to get-rich-quick schemes going awry. The 'anything goes' approach to early car design began to stabilize as a dominant configuration became the norm. Gasoline became the preferred power source over electricity and steam, while the three-wheelers and motorized dog-carts made way for what we nowadays recognize as a car: seating side by side; an enclosed engine, usually mounted in the front of a chassis; a steering wheel in place of a tiller; and pneumatic rather than solid tyres.

It was this standardization of outline that reduced the risk for many serious investors. Nonetheless, the British motor industry lagged behind its French, German and American counterparts.

Some of this was owing to the insistence on not building cars down to a price, and avoiding mass-production techniques. Through the first decade of the twentieth century, motoring became increasingly popular, but it was still beyond the means of all but a few. It was also a period that, to many people nowadays, represents an era of craftsmanship that will never be equalled. Construction of such ostentatious machinery as the original Napier and Rolls-Royce relied on a small pool of highly skilled artisans, ones who took great pride in their work.

As British marques aimed for technical perfection and individuality, the United States in particular looked to making cars in bulk using the latest production techniques. Having already inaugurated and refined many new assembly systems, Henry Ford installed a production line at the Highland Factory, near Detroit, in 1913. With this single move, mass construction became the norm, and many British manufacturers either headed further upmarket or fell by the wayside.

There was, however, an entirely new strain of popular automobile that arrived around this time that owed nothing to North America. Across Europe enterprising enthusiasts and small-volume manufacturers took their lead from the fledgling motorcycle industry, in which compact single- or twin-cylinder engines offered relative lightness and power. When mated to a skimpy chassis with equally rudimentary bodywork (often in a tandem two-seater configuration and with little weather protection), the 'cyclecar' offered motoring on a budget. What these little vehicles lacked in architectural grace and craftsmanship they more than made up for in affordability and ease of construction. Many were horrendously crude and even lethal in some instances, but the more professional offerings flourished between 1910 and the early 1920s, especially in Great Britain and France, where there was a reduced tax rate for cars weighing less than 771 lb (350 kg). Some were even offered in kit form: the British Aviette, for example, was sold as a build-your-own package for just £55. A lack of creature comforts and not much in the way of bump absorption was a small price to pay for mobility.

While the United States pioneered vehicle mass production, in Europe the perception of what represented sales volume began to shift. The economies of scale achievable from interchangeable, standardized parts and a well-drilled workforce weren't lost on British industrialists, but the investment necessary seemed justified only if vehicles could be sold in sufficient numbers to return a healthy profit. By the eve of World War I, Ford was building around 200,000 cars a year; the Wolseley Motor Company – the foremost British marque of the time – was making just 3000 a year. Manufacturers that had survived the pioneering days slowly began repositioning themselves: in order to survive, they needed to supply a variety of affordable models that would appeal to the professional classes and not just the elite.

Morgan's motorcycle-engined trikes represented the acceptable face of the short-lived cyclecar movement. Ironically, the Malvern-based marque is now one of the few genuinely autonomous British car manufacturers still in existence.

Predictably, it was Henry Ford who led the way. The American entrepreneur had established a base in Britain in 1909. The catalyst to Ford becoming a British manufacturer was the firm's import agent, Percival Perry, who realized that there would be less tax to pay as a constructor than as a concessionaire of a foreign marque. This led to the creation of the Ford Motor Company (England) in 1911, and the assembly of imported kits began at Trafford Park, near Manchester. The Model T had proved a phenomenon in the United States, and so it would prove in Europe, despite a decidedly hostile reception from the British specialist press. Built to suit the budgets of American farmers and travelling salesmen, the Model T was a low-revving, reasonably powerful contraption, designed to cover long distances in relative comfort. It was, however, a cheap and cheerful product that was met with some derision away from its homeland for being crude and ungainly.

None of this mattered to the average aspiring motorist. The Model T was an instant hit, largely because of its price. The high productivity of American parts suppliers and the efficiency of Ford's factory meant that the company could offer cars of comparable worth for less: the Model T cost roughly 25 per cent less than the equivalent Morris Oxford made by relative newcomer to the market, William Morris (later Lord Nuffield). But Detroit wasn't going to have everything its own way. The fight was only just getting started.

THE RISE AND RISE OF THE BRITISH MOTOR INDUSTRY: SMALL REALLY IS BEAUTIFUL

Like a great many British car manufacturers, the Morris marque was rooted in the bicycle trade. Having found modest success, William Morris formed WRM Motors in Oxford in 1912 with £1000 of backing from the Earl of Macclesfield. Unlike many of his contemporaries, Morris chose not to manufacture everything in-house and instead assembled cars from components bought in from outside contractors – a wise move as it enabled his company to grow rapidly without the need for substantial capital outgoings. And while it may have been undercut by the Model T, the better-made Morris Oxford soon proved to be a hit and a challenger in the market occupied by rivals Singer, Standard and Hillman. And Ford's price advantage was about to take a pummelling.

The Morris marque would emerge from World War I in a much stronger and financially more secure position than when it entered. Lucrative war contracts resulted in the Cowley factory, near Oxford,

With the 'Bullnose', Morris established itself as a major player in the fledgling British motor industry. Although it was more expensive than Ford's Model T, it was a better-made car, and it showed.

doubling in size, while enforced learning of new skills and techniques for the production of armaments, allied to the effects of using standard jigs and division of labour, were applied directly to car manufacture. Ford, meanwhile, was hit hard by a new 33 per cent tax against imports, which cut down any price advantage of using foreign parts and accelerated the need to use home-grown components. Throw in anti-American sentiment, drummed up in advertisements from local manufacturers, and Ford's progress was blunted, if only briefly.

Meanwhile, Morris soared, as did the British motor industry as a whole. In peacetime came a boom period as returning soldiers, who had experienced motorized transport probably for the first time, were anxious to spend their demobilization pay on a car of their own. Established firms found themselves competing with a whole new batch of wannabes. In a repeat of the pioneering days, there was almost a sense of gold-rush fever as every optimistic amateur with access to a garage and a proprietary engine claimed to be a manufacturer. Between 1919 and 1920 some forty new makes of car hit the market, most of them disappearing into the ether before the ink on the brochure was dry; others existed only in the fevered imagination of their designers or in share prospectuses.

As demand for cars grew, the dead wood was gradually removed, and expanded capacity and a flood of imports (regardless of protectionist tariffs) sparked cut-throat competition and price wars. It couldn't last. By 1921 the boom had collapsed as the cost of raw materials rose exponentially, labour disputes intensified, restrictions were made on hire-purchase agreements and the introduction of a tax against horsepower all conspired to dampen production. The size and scope of the industry changed dramatically over the decade, with market share comprised mostly of a few relatively large businesses catering to the mainstream and the likes of Rolls-Royce, emergent Bentley and Lagonda catering to the privileged few. The number of car manufacturers based in Great Britain in 1922 was ninety-nine. Within seven years, that figure had shrunk to just thirty-one. Morris, Singer and Austin dominated the marketplace and accounted for three-quarters of automobile production.

In the case of Austin this is all the more remarkable, as at the start of the 1920s it was staring death in the face, haemorrhaging cash and massively over-staffed. The firm's exit from World War I had differed greatly from Morris's. Austin had spent the war years building trucks, augmenting its workforce from 2000 to 22,000. In peacetime the vast expansion of premises was not easily converted into a new role. There was no money coming in, but plenty flooding out. Bankruptcy loomed. But the company was able to pay off its large debenture loans and reinvest, thanks to a brainchild of the company's instigator, Herbert Austin.

Once synonymous with motor sport, Bentley won the Le Mans 24 Hour Race five times between 1924 and 1930 (as pictured). It would be seventy-three years before the marque would triumph again in the endurance classic, by which time Bentley was owned by Volkswagen.

Despite serious doubts – and open hostility – from his own shareholders, the future Lord Austin (with the eighteen-year-old Stanley Edge) devised a diminutive sub-1-litre saloon car dubbed the Seven (see p. 39). Introduced in 1922, it proved to be a major hit, remaining in production for seventeen years. Between 1929 and 1933 the British share in world car exports rose from 7 to 25 per cent, much of this increase being due to Austin. And aside from the Seven saving the Austin name and allowing the company to prosper as a major industrial player, its arrival led to ramifications that not even its mastermind could have foreseen.

The Seven mobilized the British populace like no other car. At a stroke it killed off the cyclecar movement. At only £165 it was just as cheap; plus, it was better made, could seat four and was easier to maintain. But, more than anything, the Seven ultimately played its own small part in establishing overseas marques, the very same ones that would ultimately consume the British motor industry. When BMW took over Rover (formerly Austin-Rover) in 1994, the irony wasn't lost on many bystanders: the Bayerische Motoren Werke's first car, the Dixi 3/15PS, had been an Austin Seven made under licence.

The Seven was also built in France and North America, and helped to establish the Japanese motor industry, too, however unwittingly. Nissan's Type 15 was a close crib of the Seven, much to the chagrin of Herbert Austin. Another far-reaching – and improbable – consequence of this car's existence was the formation of the post-war British production racing-car industry. The Seven's availability, affordability and ease of tuning led to the formation of the 750 Motor Club in 1939. Its future alumni would include such names as Colin Chapman (Lotus) and Eric Broadley (Lola) among others, who would change the face of motor sport in the 1950s, 1960s and beyond.

ONWARDS, UPWARDS AND SIDEWAYS: BRITANNIA RULES THE ROADS

The 1930s can be viewed as a dividing line, when traditional coachbuilding was superseded by mass-produced cars with pressed-steel bodies. This was also the decade when most of the few remaining autonomous marques lost their independence. Morris had purchased the bankrupt Wolseley in 1926 and followed through by taking over the small but respected Riley concern in 1938. Vauxhall, hitherto a maker of luxury sporting cars, had become part of the vast General Motors combine in 1925 and turned to pursuing mediocrity with remarkable conviction. Meanwhile, Humber, Hillman and Commer merged under the Rootes banner.

In a relatively short period of time the motor industry had proved its importance to the British economy. By the late 1930s it had become the largest of its kind in Europe, buoyed by middle-class incomes and a degree of governmental protectionism. Yet its significance to the nation's financial well-being was to prove just as vital as a provider of military hardware. By 1936 five of the largest motor manufacturers had set up 'shadow factories' that could be used to build aero engines in the event of war. Production of Jeeps, tanks, bomber aircraft and boats once hostilities broke out in 1939 meant that the automobile industry's role in the war effort was beyond measure, despite Coventry – the country's industrial hub and home of most major car manufacturers – taking an almighty battering.

This stoicism would be severely tested once fighting ended in 1945. Despite being beleaguered by shortages of raw materials and a degree of outside interference, the British motor industry soon found its feet. Demand for new cars – any car – was huge, but governmental controls channelled the supply of steel to firms that exported 50 per cent of their production (75 per cent from 1947). To counter greedy speculators buying new cars and then selling them on with a hefty mark-up, customers had to sign a contract guaranteeing that they would not resell within twelve months.

The national motor industries in France and Germany had suffered more and took considerably longer to regroup, owing to the effects of defeat, occupation, division or devaluation, and British firms were all too happy to exploit the situation. Export sales surged as demand from Europe and North America witnessed record production figures. Add in Commonwealth countries, where there was a ready-made market, and it isn't difficult to see why Britain suddenly found itself as the world's premier car exporter. In 1937 its share of world car exports was 15 per cent. By 1950 it had more than tripled, to 52 per cent, with vehicle production being one-third greater than on the eve of World War II.

This remarkable achievement would not last. By the mid-1950s Detroit players were satisfying home demand while Germany bounced back to overtake France in terms of volume manufacture. By the end of the decade, Germany had also overtaken Great Britain, and its dominance of the European automobile market was only just getting started.

It's hard to believe that Vauxhall, a marque renowned for its mass-produced – and often deathly dull – saloons and hatchbacks, ushered in the sports car with the Prince Henry. The C-type of 1911 is shown here.

CULT OF THE SPORTS CAR, AND REACHING THE TIPPING POINT

The 1950s witnessed dramatic – and occasionally traumatic – shifts in the way the British motor industry operated that would, in time, lead to its ruination. Yet this was also the decade in which Britain produced many landmark designs that left foreign rivals trailing in their wake and established a level of dominance in motor sport that has yet to subside.

By 1952 American-owned marques Ford and Vauxhall accounted for 29 per cent of British car sales. That same year, after much persuasion (about twenty-five years' worth), Lord Nuffield (né William Morris) agreed to merge his empire – Morris, MG, Riley and Wolseley – with that of the Austin Motor Company. In a single move the new British Motor Corporation consolidated its combined 40 per cent market share, but it was widely viewed internally as a shotgun wedding. Each side had long-established operating procedures and infrastructures, and unifying the two former rival organizations proved a formidable task. Some, including Leonard Lord, managing director of BMC, viewed the merger as a victory attributable to Austin's waiting game (Lord Nuffield was seventy-five years old by this time). This mindset among senior personnel, allied to deeply held and long-nurtured animosity among former opponents, led to a predictable lack of communication and wilful obstruction between divisions. The situation would, if anything, only get worse over time.

It didn't help that the cars being produced by BMC were so underwhelming. Demand was still high because of scarcity, and the phrase 'export or die' became seared into the collective consciousness. Yet the conglomerate's ability to squeeze every last pound, peso, yen or dollar out of a model that had long ceased to charm was truly extraordinary – and short-sighted. To make matters worse, a laissez-faire attitude to rationalizing the product range didn't extend much beyond reducing the number of engines being used across the board. Some models overlapped, competing for the same customers, and BMC began producing the same car but with different marque and model names. This 'badge engineering' approach to design saw many once-proud makes of car reduced to glorified 'de luxe' packages, and it fooled nobody. Distributors and dealers continued to act as separate sales outlets, which only added to competition within the company. Instead of creating new purpose-built factories for mass manufacture, BMC duplicated production lines within existing antiquated sites. Product pricing was still largely done by 'guesstimation', and less than 1 per cent of turnover was used for research and development. This lack of foresight would prove catastrophic.

Yet for all the apathy and autocratic management, the British automobile industry was still capable of building hugely accomplished motor cars, even if it was generally left to subdivisions or niche manufacturers to realize them. MG in particular proved the concept of the Everyman sports car.

Although almost as old as the automobile itself, the concept or rationale behind sports cars has changed seismically since the tag was applied to the first vehicle to wear the moniker: the Vauxhall C-type Prince Henry of 1911. Back then, such a car was beyond the means of all but the super-rich and was intended primarily for competition – sport, as the appellation suggests. Perhaps more by accident than by design, MG took the basic notion and made it a hugely populist one. From a first toe-in-the-water exercise in 1923, Morris Garages would propagate all manner of different models, and it was the MG TC Midget (see p. 97) that introduced North America to the sports-car ideal in the immediate post-war years. Despite the company having no official presence across the Atlantic, and the TC having no left-hand-drive configuration, around 2000 of the cars headed Stateside. The TC's top speed of 77 mph (124 km/h) rendered it slower than the average Buick, Oldsmobile or other Detroit saloon car, but its responsiveness in corners more than made up for this. Enthusiasm for this 'fun car' undoubtedly had a major effect on the birth of road racing in the United States, with early customers including future Formula One world champion Phil Hill, along with fellow American ace John Fitch. The TD model was an even bigger smash: in 1952 the ratio of numbers exported to those sold at home was an extraordinary forty-two to one.

MG didn't have everything its own way. From within BMC the T-series faced a stiff challenge from the altogether more modern Austin-Healey 100 (see p. 144 for the 100S), while rival Standard-Triumph followed its lacklustre 1800 roadster with the rugged (some might say agricultural) TR2, which was considerably faster and more agile.

During the 1950s, with such cars as the DBR1, Aston Martin became a respected player in endurance racing under David Brown's custodianship, culminating with victory in the 1959 Le Mans 24 Hour Race and that year's World Sports Car Championship title.

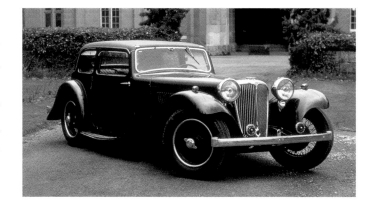

Based on Standard running gear, the SSI of 1931, Jaguar's first foray into automobile manufacture, was just the opening salvo in a canon of (mostly) beautiful cars.

Founded in 1956 by Peter Pellandine, Falcon Shells was a prolific supplier of kit-car bodies to 'specials' builders. Its glassfibre bodyshells also appeared on early Elva racing cars and a factory-entered Austin-Healey Le Mans car.

Swimming away from the mainstream sports cars were the many specialist marques. Jaguar (originally called SS but renamed because of Nazi connotations) in particular helped redefine the genre, slackening jaws with the XK120 (see p. 111). When launched at the 1948 London Motor Show, this almost pornographic vision of automotive magnificence ushered in a decade of performance vehicles from Jaguar that culminated with five wins in the Le Mans 24 Hour Race during the 1950s with the closely related C- and D-type models (see pp. 121 and 150).

A mite less dazzling was the Italianate Ace (see p. 133) from Thames Ditton minnow AC Cars. This firm, which had roots in three-wheeled delivery vehicles, would ultimately find great fame in the 1960s with the Cobra roadster (see p. 198). More rarefied still was the DB2 from Aston Martin (see p. 117), the marque having been saved from extinction by tractor magnate David Brown (Sir David from 1968). Having spotted an advertisement in *The Times* in the autumn of 1946, he bought the company for £25,000 and then snapped up the equally calamitous Lagonda months later for £52,500; he then set about taking the fight to Continental rivals with a raft of GTs and racing cars. Alongside Jaguar, Aston Martin did much to instil pride in British sporting achievement by winning the 1959 Le Mans 24 Hour Race with the DBR1 and the World Sportscar Championship the same year.

All of this was fine for those who could afford such machines. For those impecunious enthusiasts who could not, the 1950s witnessed the birth of a new subspecies of automobile that was the answer to their prayers: the kit car. With the vast majority of new vehicles heading overseas, and a paucity of good second-hand cars, enterprising enthusiasts took to building these 'specials'. While the concept of a home-built car was not in itself an entirely new phenomenon, the birth of a new-fangled wonder material, glassfibre, undoubtedly had a huge effect on the explosion of new manufacturers aiming their wares at budding self-builders. Bodyshells could be built cheaply and in volume by just about anyone, and the proliferation of offerings – nearly all of them sports cars – was staggering.

That said, the term 'kit car' is a bit of a misnomer, as the vast majority were little more than bare bodies intended, more often than not, to be mated with Austin Seven or pre-war Ford Ten running gear. Quite often, instructions would consist of little more than expressionistic diagrams and a few pages of vague directions, such as 'attach body to chassis'. And that was if instructions were included at all. Yet the can-do spirit behind the 'specials' boom resulted in some fairly accomplished machines. A rebodied Austin Seven would probably seem comical to many, but the ingenuity invested in a great many examples of this breed resulted in cars that provided genuinely sporting behaviour. The proliferation of performance-enhancing equipment that arrived at this time to cater for kit builders undoubtedly played a major role in establishing the aftermarket tuning industry, while a great many of the specials manufacturers, at least the ones that outlived the 1950s, would go on to move upmarket and take on the major players.

Perhaps the ultimate specials builder – and one who effectively pre-dated and inspired the movement – was Anthony Colin Bruce Chapman. The word 'genius' is bandied around with monotonous regularity but, with regard to this brilliant designer and motivational force, it truly did apply. A visionary, and never one to fear experimentation, Chapman was studying engineering at University College London when he constructed a trials car – retrospectively known as Lotus Mk1 – around the remains of an old Austin Seven. When completed in 1948, it proved moderately successful, and motor sport was to take over Chapman's life. Within ten years, he had bested all-comers in domestic sports racing, and pioneered the use of a glassfibre monocoque with the gorgeous Lotus Elite coupé (see p. 158).

For Colin Chapman road cars were always a means to an end, a method of raising revenue to fund his competition endeavours. For much of the 1950s British hopes had rested with BRM (British Racing Motors). Unfortunately, the Bourne équipe consistently underperformed at Grand Prix level, while rival

Always the innovator, Lotus founder Colin Chapman was forever searching for the next big thing. The Eleven, seen here (produced from 1956 to 1958), was the culmination of his relationship with Irish-born aerodynamicist Frank Costin. Its light weight and streamlined form meant that it was outrageously quick, even with a small displacement engine.

Vanwall bested the might of Italian and German teams only to pull out almost as quickly as it appeared. It was Surbiton *garagistes* (as Enzo Ferrari famously, and dismissively, referred to them) Charles and John Cooper who turned the racing world on its head. They moved the engine behind the driver – or horse behind the cart (Ferrari again …) – to win the 1959 and 1960 Formula One world drivers' and constructors' championships. The team soon faded, but Lotus picked up from where the Coopers left off. With the occasional diversion, such as changing the face of Champ Car racing in the United States by winning the 1965 Indy 500 with a mid-engined design, Lotus consistently uprooted goalposts and ran away with them. From Stirling Moss's victory in the 1961 Monaco Grand Prix in Rob Walker's privateer Lotus 18, to the marque's final Formula One appearance in 1994, Lotus accrued an astounding seventy-nine overall wins and six drivers' titles – a remarkable achievement considering the marque's humble ancestry.

AUSTERITY MOTORING, BIRTH OF AN ICON AND MERGE, MERGE, MERGE …

While the specials movement displayed a very British can-do spirit and a novel means of recycling an old car into an altogether different one, an entirely new strain of budget automobile gained centre stage in the second half of the 1950s: the microcar. Maverick engineer Laurie Bond had already provided cheap transport with his eponymous three-wheelers. These crude, motorcycle-powered devices were irredeemably ugly and lacking in any real technical merit, but they were cheap and sold in reasonable numbers, all the more so following the Suez Canal debacle.

During the colonial era (and in particular after the Anglo-Egyptian Treaty of 1936), the Suez Canal, through which two-thirds of Europe's oil was imported, had been controlled by Great Britain. In 1951 Egypt insisted on the canal's return to Egyptian hands, and by 1954 the Britain agreed to pull out. But plans began to unravel in 1956 after the Egyptian leader, Gamal Abdel Nasser, nationalized the Suez Canal Company, bringing oil shipments to a halt. Ultimately, the crisis resulted in the resignation of the prime minister, Sir Anthony Eden.

For the British motorist the Suez Crisis resulted in austerity measures and soaring oil prices. Microcars suddenly made sense. It was largely such foreign machines as the Italian Isetta and German Messerschmidt, however, that popularized the microcar (or 'bubble car'). Characterful though they may have been, these tiny vehicles were generally primitive and hateful to drive. One onlooker who especially loathed them was Alexander (Alec) Issigonis. Having already been instrumental in creating the first British car ever to sell more than one million units – the much-loved Morris Minor – he issued a retort to these ungodly motorcycle-powered contraptions that would prove even more influential.

Jaguar's XJ saloons, introduced in 1968, were arguably the best cars of any kind available anywhere in the world at the time, offering pace, beauty and remarkable value for money. Unfortunately, with Jaguar having become mired in the British Leyland combine, build quality would take a bruising, as would the manufacturer's reputation.

The Austin Se7en Mini or Morris Mini Cooper – or simply Mini (see p. 169) – was a truly modern small car. Introduced in 1959, it was revolutionary thanks to its space-saving layout of transverse engine and front-wheel drive. Here was a car that was affordable, mass-produced, fun to drive; it was perhaps the world's first classless car. Although initially the Mini was a slow seller, demand for it soon took off as the 1960s started swinging. It didn't much matter that it had only sliding windows and a sash-pull cord for opening the doors; such quirks were of little consequence in an accessible small car that endeared itself to everyone regardless of background. Throw in the various performance-enhanced Cooper editions that scooped British and European saloon-car championships as well as three Monte Carlo Rally wins, and the Mini's cult status was assured. Suddenly a leaky, draughty, slow microcar didn't seem so appealing.

Unfortunately, for all its vision, the Mini was never profitable. Allowed virtually free rein during the planning phase, Issigonis was blissfully unburdened by cost implications, but blazing trails is rarely lucrative. Ford's rival 105E Anglia was an altogether more conventional car that sold in large numbers and returned a profit. Ford's UK manager of product planning, Sir Terence Beckett, had a Mini stripped down for cost-analysis purposes and deduced that for the £496 asking price BMC was losing £30 on each car. And it wasn't just the Mini. The similar but larger 1100/1300 range (variously offered with Austin, Morris, MG, Riley and Vanden Plas badging) was also super-successful on the showroom floor but made only a negative return on investment.

If the rot had already set in, few noticed. The 1960s witnessed coalescence of the British motor industry that was to have a far-reaching effect on the nation. The possibility of restructuring and reorganizing the industry was discussed at the highest governmental level, and the creation of one principal automotive superpower kicked off in 1961, when commercial-vehicle manufacturer Leyland Motors bought out Standard-Triumph, having already taken over rival truck builders Scammell and Albion. The firm had hitherto failed as a car manufacturer (Leyland had briefly made luxury cars between 1920 and 1923), and this re-entry into building automobiles was just the opening salvo as its sustained shopping spree netted Rover (having already funded its gas-turbine research) and its Alvis subsidiary in 1967. Leyland now owned several marques that covered bases in sports cars, saloon cars and off-roaders (through Land-Rover), but none was robust financially despite dominating particular niches.

In Coventry Jaguar had bounced back from a potentially catastrophic fire at its Browns Lane factory in February 1957 to launch the E-type four years later (see p. 184). Perhaps *the* automotive icon of its day, this was a supercar before the term had even been coined (although only cars given to the press achieved the advertised 150 mph/241 km/h). As the standard-bearer of accessible high-performance sports and saloon cars, Jaguar had been on its own spending binge, taking over rival Daimler in 1960, followed by lorry firm Guy and proprietary engine manufacturers Meadows and Coventry Climax. Then in 1965 BMC went on the offensive and put the back up just about every motor-industry supremo, not least Jaguar's Sir William Lyons: it took over Pressed Steel, a major supplier of bodyshells and engineering to most key manufacturers. Pressed Steel was the sole source of Jaguar panels. Keen to safeguard his company's future, and having so far fended off unwanted takeover bids, including one from Leyland Motors, Lyons led Jaguar's merger with BMC in 1966 to form the new juggernaut, British Motor Holdings (BMH). Lyons was now a partner in a massive organization that encompassed Austin, Morris, Wolseley and Riley among others.

BMH would last only two years; another altogether bigger merger was looming. The British government under Labour premier Harold Wilson was keen to rationalize and consolidate the British motor industry; it was, after all, the largest manufacturing exporter and, prior to devaluation in 1967, vital to economic policy. It was also a significant employer.

The idea of merging BMH with Leyland Motors was first floated by the minister of technology, Tony Benn. Directors of BMH were initially reluctant to commit, but formal pressure was applied through the Industrial Reorganisation Corporation, a governmental body that aimed to restructure British industry. Following personal intervention by the prime minister, who claimed that such a merger was in the national interest, the two monoliths merged in 1968 to form British Leyland Motor Holdings, soon renamed British Leyland Motor Corporation (BLMC).

TROUBLE, STRIFE AND A COMMON ENEMY

Away from the hard-nosed, big-business end of the British motor industry, the minnows and small fry weren't exactly flourishing. The specialist sports-car movement that had grown out of the specials era had progressively withered away as economies of scale made it nearly impossible to compete head-on with volume producers. A loophole that meant a 66 per cent reduction in purchase tax for cars in kit form was also plugged and, at a stroke, all price advantages were lost.

At the altogether more rarefied end of the market, AC Cars was effectively dormant as the 1970s dawned, with only tiny numbers of its pretty 428 Maserati lookalike being made (see p. 220), owing to an unreliable Italian subcontractor. Aston Martin, meanwhile, had pressed ahead with its DBS model and an all-new V8 engine, and was prospering under David Brown's stewardship. For him sports cars were still essentially a non-profitable diversion away from the serious business of making tractors and gears, but there was more kudos to be found in having your initials attached to a luxury grand tourer car than on a mud-plugging farm instrument. Nonetheless, after he had placed his son Christopher in charge of the David Brown Group in 1969, the business lost £10 million in eighteen months. Needing to divest itself of revenue-sapping distractions, the Newport Pagnell firm sold off Aston Martin Lagonda in 1972 for the nominal price of £1000 – plus the company's debts, which totalled an estimated £5 million. Its new custodianship would prove fleeting, as the firm lurched into receivership in late 1974. A rescue bid by an international consortium fended off the inevitable as a tie-in with MG for a smaller, cheaper model died a death in the late 1970s. In 1981 the firm was saved by Pace Petroleum's boss, Victor Gauntlett.

That great paragon of British automotive excellence, Rolls-Royce (and its Bentley sister marque), similarly faced an uphill struggle. While the company was producing more cars than ever before, thanks largely to the 'entry-level' Silver Shadow model, and returning a profit, problems encountered with an aero-engine contract caused the business to lurch into receivership in late 1970. In May of the following year a new company – Rolls-Royce Motors – was floated. It was to concentrate on car manufacture and

It's come to this ... Triumph's last car was the Acclaim, a British-made Honda produced from 1981 to 1984. It was a good car, and paved the way for a generation of Rovers, but it proved beyond all doubt that Britain's role as the axis of automobile manufacture was over.

would remain independent until being bought out by engineering group Vickers in August 1980. While the blue-chip end of the market fluctuated between relative prosperity and downward plunge, the unwieldy BLMC behemoth struggled with a mix of lacklustre products, reluctant rationalization and in-fighting among former rival groups. But all the disparate factions found a common enemy in Sir Donald Stokes, the new man in charge, who came to be seen as a whipping boy by MG enthusiasts for seemingly favouring Triumph, and by Mini enthusiasts for sidelining Alec Issigonis. Stokes inherited a sprawling mess of clapped-out factories rife with seemingly untenable labour problems. The number of stoppages in the motor industry through walkouts had increased tenfold between 1948 and 1973, yet the concept of mass redundancies that would follow rationalization was unthinkable to a Labour government, and Stokes wasn't about to be its hatchet man.

Predictably, the firm collapsed in 1975, only to be bailed out by the government to the tune of £2.4 billion. The newly reminted British Leyland was still plagued with labour unrest, much of it centred on Derek Robinson, a union shop steward who had greater control over BL than any manager: through his network of union leaders he could close factories as if on a whim. In a bid to curb union power, South African-born troubleshooter Sir Michael Edwards was brought in. Having accrued evidence of Robinson's Communist links, he dismissed 'Red Robbo' in 1979. Edwards then began a ruthless programme of factory closures, the biggest casualties being MG's assembly plant in Abingdon and Triumph facilities in Speke and Canley. A real masterstroke was a tie-in with Honda, Japan's third-largest car manufacturer at the time, which led to the joint development of a range of cars. With BL suitably fortified, Jaguar was privatized to become a standalone marque in 1984, while a takeover bid the following year by Ford for what was now called Austin-Rover (the Morris brand was dropped in 1983, Triumph twelve months later) was rebuffed by the Conservative premier, Margaret Thatcher.

The firm (Rover Group from 1986) was instead taken over by British Aerospace in 1988 (with Honda taking a 20 per cent stake) for a grossly undervalued sum of £150 million plus a £520 million dowry. By 1991 Rover was making just 400,000 cars a year. A subsequent sell-off to BMW in 1994 for a whopping £800 million saw the arrival of an all-important new model, the Rover 75. It was beautifully made but looked like a car your grandfather would drive, and failed to find favour. After hiving off the Mini brand, BMW sold the business to the Phoenix Consortium in 2000 for the grand sum of £10. Apart from a major repositioning of the MG brand, thanks to high-profile motor-sport involvement, the firm achieved little other than to blow £500 million of BMW 'sweeteners' before its last gasp in 2005. What passed for assets were bought by the Chinese Nanjing Automobile Group.

It could have been good, but it wasn't. With the TR7, produced between 1974 and 1981, Triumph under British Leyland well and truly lost its way. The car was styled by Harris Mann, and its radical wedge shape wasn't unattractive. Unfortunately, however, it was thrown together and lacked the level of performance expected of a TR-series sports car.

IS THERE A FUTURE FOR THE BRITISH MOTOR INDUSTRY?

Having reached so many peaks, the British motor industry is presently in a trough and is unlikely ever to scale the giddy heights of fifty years ago, or even come close. Globalization and the high cost of manufacture in Great Britain almost certainly count against it. There are some slivers of hope, however. Since buying Jaguar in 1989 for US$2.5 million, Ford has sunk a further US$5 billion into propping it up and ensuring its survival. With the new XK range, and industry-leading build quality, Jaguar may finally stop bleeding red ink. Only its parent company's perilous financial state could pull the rug from under it. What was Ford's other slice of British performance-car heritage, Aston Martin (bought in 1987), has gone from last rites to Ferrari-baiting success, even if the coachbuilt nature of the cars has been quietly dropped in favour of mass production. In March 2007 Ford sold the firm for US$925 million to a consortium headed by accountant turned motor-sport entrepreneur David Richards. It may conceivably also hive off its Land-Rover brand, the premier off-roader marque (plus sister marque Range Rover), which it bought from BMW in 2000 for £1.85 billion following the break-up of Rover.

Meanwhile, Rolls-Royce and Bentley are under the protective cloak of German owners. In 1997 Vickers chose to sell both sister brands and, after many negotiations, BMW announced itself as victor in 1998, only to be outfoxed by Volkswagen. Ultimately, BMW got control of Rolls-Royce, and Bentley passed to its rival. Both marques have flourished under their respective guardians, even if their products lack that intangible quality of 'Britishness'.

Of the more populist brands, MG may yet make a comeback as Nanjing reboots production in Britain, but the future of the industry – at least as an indigenous entity – lies with the tiddlers. Morgan, which has outwardly bypassed the industry machinations by ploughing its own singular furrow since 1910, is currently enjoying success in overseas markets, while the AC brand is being reanimated from the vestiges of the defunct Mercedes-Benz-backed Smart Roadster. Other small-scale manufacturers, such as Ariel, Radical and Noble, have all proved that there is a market for bespoke, track-orientated sports cars, while perennial coffin-dodger Lotus has somehow survived serial ownership to produce more landmark designs, such as the hugely popular Elise.

Either way, Great Britain still has an automotive brains trust that is the envy of the world, one that is more than capable of producing new legends. And while there may be few native marques left to support, the British motor industry is far from dead. It's just pared back and sleeping off a hangover.

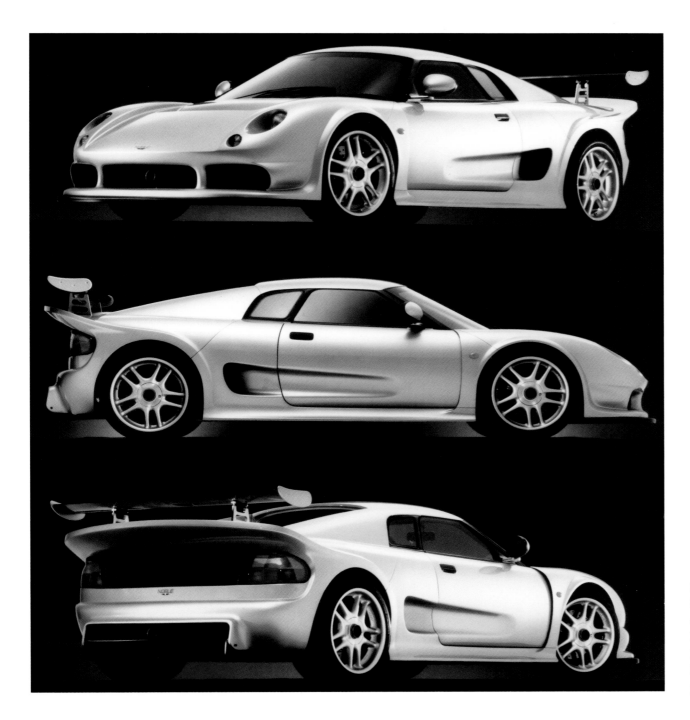

Britain's great white hope? Noble has been one of Britain's great sports-car success stories in recent years (seen here is the Noble M12, introduced in 2001), with much of its componentry being made abroad. Will the marque prosper? Only time will tell ...

BRITISH AUTO LEGENDS

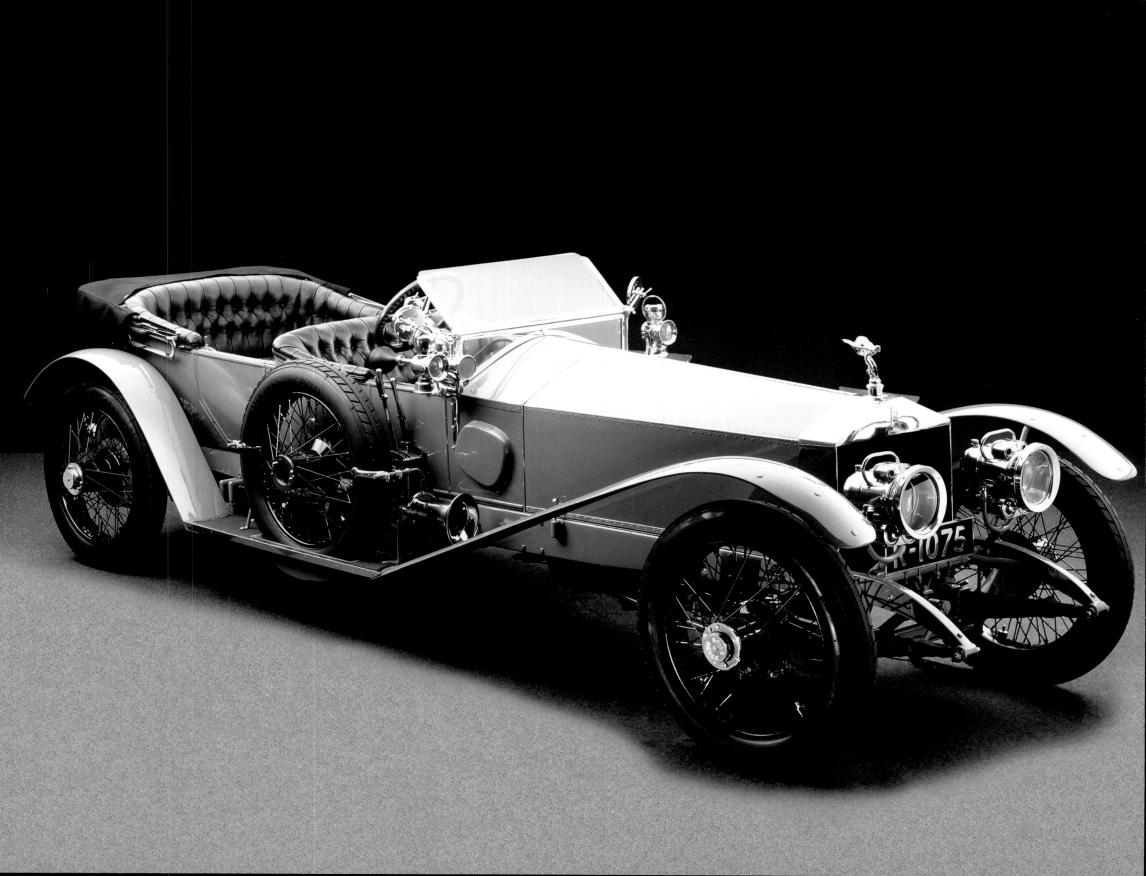

ROLLS-ROYCE SILVER GHOST

It was the car for which a new word was coined: waftability. Introduced in 1907, at a time when the preferred mode of transport was still a horse and cart, the Rolls-Royce 40–50 HP was simply the finest car offered on sale anywhere. *The Autocar* described the sensation of being driven in the six-cylinder leviathan as like 'being wafted through the countryside ... the smoothest thing we have ever experienced'. Massively over-engineered and effortlessly powerful, it set the template for all future models, and waftability became an in-house maxim.

The twelfth car made had its coachwork finished in aluminium paint and was swiftly dubbed the 'Silver Ghost'. The name was subsequently adopted as an official designation, with outside coachbuilders only enhancing the legend with striking outlines that mirrored the inherent technical excellence. The model's reliability was exemplary: in 1907 one Silver Ghost was driven for forty days and nights and ran faultlessly over a distance of 14,371 miles (23,127 km). A challenge from rival Napier in 1911 involving a drive from London to Edinburgh followed by a high-speed run at the Brooklands circuit in Surrey saw the Rolls-Royce average 24.3 mpg (8.6 km per litre) and attain 78.2 mph (125.8 km/h); the Napier managed 19.3 mpg (6.8 km per litre) and 76.4 mph (123 km/h). In 1913 the Silver Ghost added to its lustre by dominating the Alpine Trial and winning the Spanish Grand Prix.

Almost as famous as the car itself is its mascot, the Spirit of Ecstasy. She was created in 1911 when artist Charles Sykes was commissioned to illustrate a sales brochure. The figurine, of a young woman with arms outstretched, gown flowing in her wake, was originally called the Spirit of Speed and was made only because owners were fitting their own individual mascots, some of which the car's makers deemed inappropriate to a car of such stature. It has adorned every Rolls-Royce since.

Drivers of the Silver Ghost kept their minds focused by having to master the ignition advance/retard control mounted in the centre of the steering wheel.

Opposite: The Silver Ghost was the epitome of quality British workmanship. It defined the lofty standards that were expected of Rolls-Royce and proved to be a hard act to follow.

Right: The cabin was perhaps a mite 'cosy', but the folding windscreen allowed the occupants to experience an exhilarating sensation of speed.

Left: Precision instruments enabled the owner – or chauffeur – of a Silver Ghost to monitor accurately the engine's performance and requirements.

Opposite: Rolls-Royce engineering wasn't at the vanguard of new ideas, but smoothness and reliability were significant benefits of the firm's exquisite attention to detail.

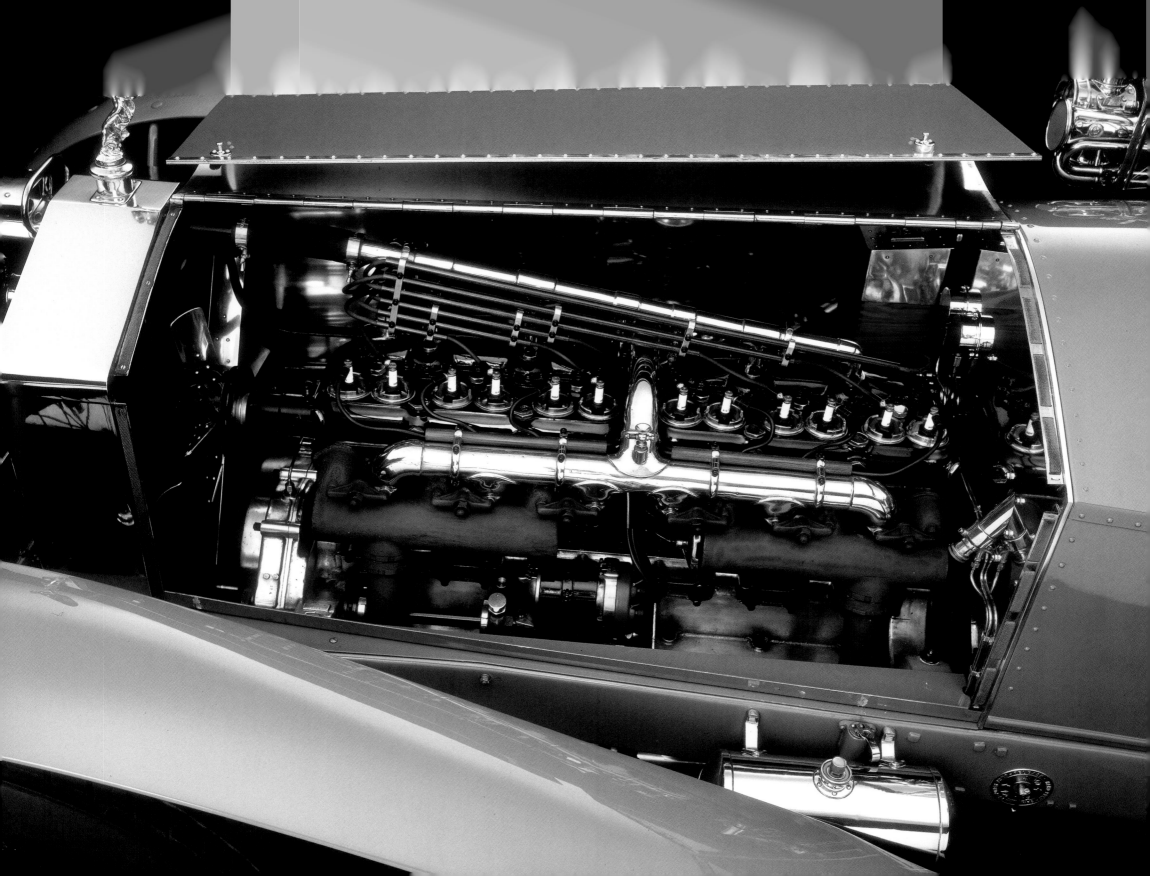

With the folding roof erected, some
of the Silver Ghost's elegance is lost.
Tension straps needed to be fastened
across the front wings to keep the
roof in place when the car was
moving at speed.

1922 AUSTIN SEVEN

For a car of such small dimensions, the Seven cast a long shadow. Introduced in 1922, this tiny vehicle – overall length was just 8 ft 10 in. (2692 mm) – turned Austin's flagging fortunes around and left an indelible mark on automotive history. Company principal Herbert Austin was all too aware of the Ford Model T's phenomenal sales success and firmly believed that a smaller, lighter but equally affordable rival would be a surefire winner. Many senior personnel were less than convinced by his scheme, however, and it took Austin's threat of handing over the design to competitor (and his former employer) Wolseley to earn their begrudging accord.

One of the most significant cars of the pre-war era regardless of nationality, the Seven saved Austin and helped establish several overseas marques.

The car's make-up was disarmingly simple. The Seven weighed just 794 lb (360 kg), and its tiny 696-cc (later 747-cc) sidevalve engine initially produced a modest 10.5 bhp. The front end was suspended by a transverse leaf spring, and there were two quarter-elliptic springs at the rear; on early cars there was nothing as superfluous or unnecessary as shock absorbers. Remaining faithful to its original rationale of affordable transport, the Seven received several improvements along the way, and by the time production ended in 1939 around 220,000 had been made.

Although the model was primarily sold in the home market, it was of immeasurable importance on a global scale. The Seven was built under licence in France by Rosengart, was the first car constructed by BMW (as the Dixi) and, in a roundabout way, helped establish the Japanese automobile industry, since Nissan cribbed the design wholesale for its Type 15 model. Jaguar's roots are also firmly entwined with the Seven, as marque-founder Sir William Lyons created coachbuilt variants under the Swallow banner before becoming a fully fledged car manufacturer himself. What's more, Colin Chapman built his first Lotus using a Seven as a basis, and established a legend in the process. Others followed his lead and in doing so created the British production racing car industry, something not even Herbert Austin could ever have envisaged.

Opposite: Stark but efficient, the Seven was rudimentary at best but a step up from contemporary cyclecars, which offered even less in the way of comfort.

Left: The tiny four-cylinder engine proved remarkably resilient and offered great tuning potential. Austin raced its own Seven-based machine with a twin-cam cylinder head, while such marques as Lotus started out using Seven engines.

Left: Narrow track and spindly tyres meant that the Seven's road-holding could be treacherous when the car was pushed hard, but it was rugged and a great starting point for early 'specials' builders.

Opposite: Able to carry four people in relative comfort, the Seven was a true 'people's car'. It was subsequently made under licence in France, Germany and North America, and was also cribbed by Nissan.

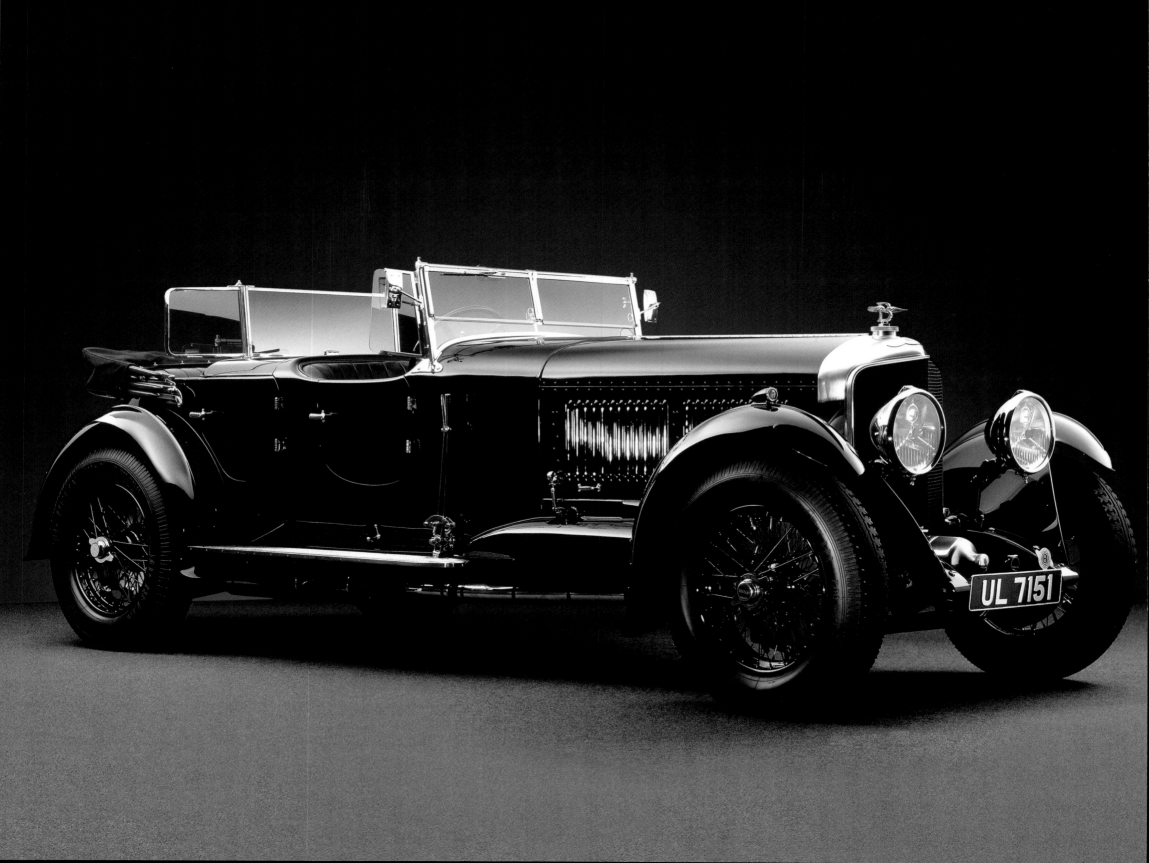

1926 BENTLEY 6½-LITRE/SPEED SIX

It was somehow appropriate that Walter Owen Bentley (universally known as W.O.) earned his engineering schooling from working on locomotives. What his eponymous creations lacked in architectural grace they more than made up for in mass. Bentleys – or rather those cars that pre-dated the Rolls-Royce acquisition – were the ultimate British sports cars of their day, diametrically opposed in ethos to the spindly Continental fare they routinely vanquished in the Le Mans 24 Hour Race. For much of the 1920s, the Circuit de la Sarthe was the marque's spiritual home, with five wins between 1924 and 1930. Bentleys were vast, perpendicular and improbably quick: rival Ettore Bugatti caustically labelled them 'the fastest lorries on earth'.

While Bentleys from this period are commonly pictured with racing-style bodywork, coachbuilt outlines were commonplace. And it was their heft that led to the creation of the 6½-litre. A prototype was extensively tested in France in 1925, and a chance encounter with an experimental Rolls-Royce Phantom convinced W.O. that he needed to devise a larger displacement engine: production cars would feature a 6597-cc straight-six with a then highly unusual arrangement of four valves per cylinder housed in a variety of wheelbases, from 11 ft (3352 mm) to an enormous 12 ft 6 in. (3810 mm). In no way were Bentleys small.

In 1928 a more overtly sporting version was introduced, with a higher compression ratio and twin SU carburettors. The Speed Six was the ultimate competition-inspired Bentley and claimed the last two wins at Le Mans for the marque (until the Audi-backed challenger in 2003). This vindicated W.O. Bentley's belief that a normally aspirated car would be a safer and more reliable bet than a supercharged one. Production lasted until 1930, by which time 545 cars had been made, 182 of them Speed Sixes.

A motoring name with a fabulous heritage, Bentley had been a prolific winner in endurance events before becoming the marque of choice for plutocrats.

Imposing, emphatic and built along the principle that bigger is better, the 6½-litre was a formidable competition tool and brought glory to Britain in motor sport in the late 1920s.

Below: While possibly lacking the jewel-like sophistication of rival Bugattis, the 6½-litre had power and reliability in its armoury.

Opposite: The massive overhead-cam straight-six engine was relatively sophisticated for its day, having four valves – and two spark plugs – per cylinder.

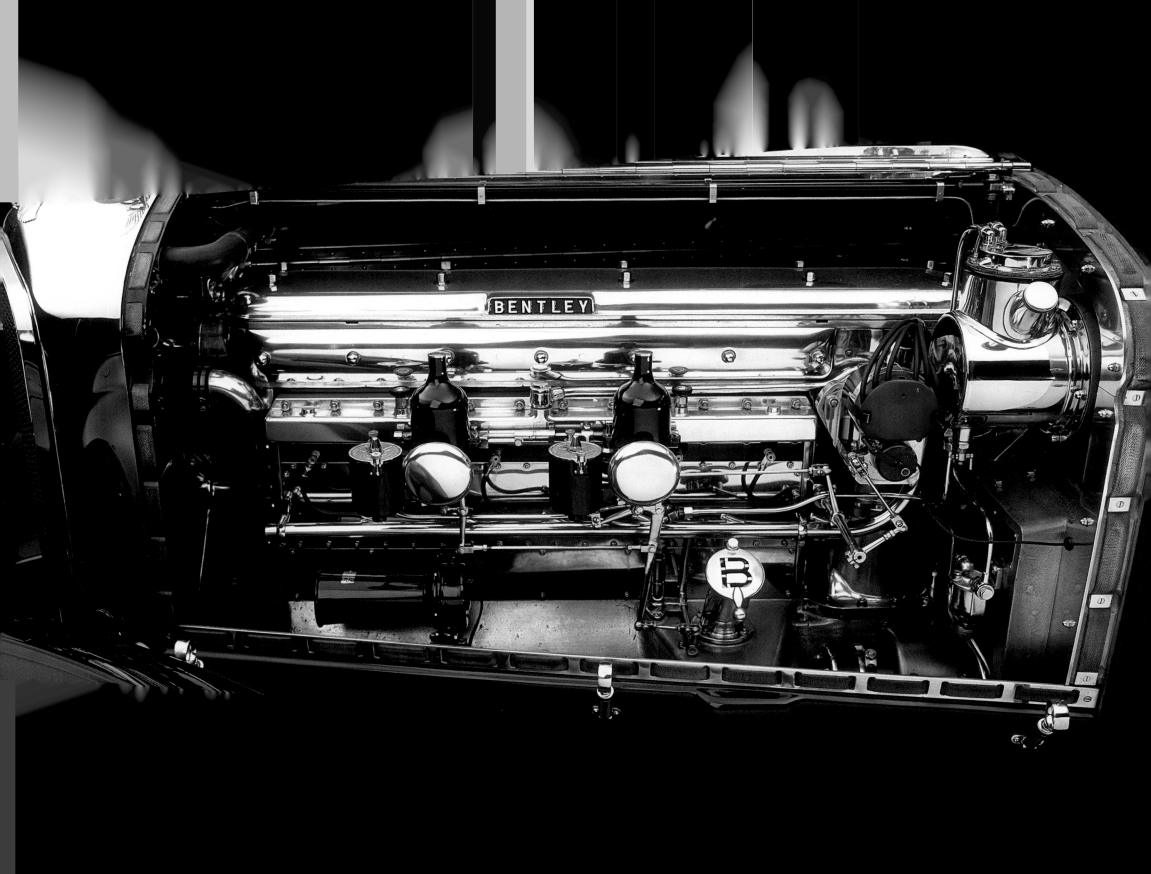

Opposite: This fabulous Speed Six from 1926 was bodied by Vanden Plas and used as a demonstrator by the then well-known Bentley agents Kensington Moir & Straker.

Below: The cabin is well equipped for its era, with plentiful instrumentation. Brakes are adjustable from the cockpit. Rear passengers have their own screen to restrict airflow and buffeting.

1929 BENTLEY 4½-LITRE SUPERCHARGED

It was a car that singularly failed to live up to expectations, and you could argue that the esteem in which the 'Blower' Bentley (so-called because of its supercharged engine) is still held is out of all proportion to its true worth. But that would be to miss the point entirely. While it was never very successful in motor racing, to legions of worshippers this particular strain of Bentley is a symbol of a lost empire, one where fact and legend merge.

It is therefore ironic that marque-founder W.O. Bentley was dismissive of the model; in fact, he hated it. Having dominated the Le Mans 24 Hour Race for much of the 1920s, Bentleys were supercars before the term had even been coined. In a bid to keep the brand at the sharp end of motor racing, driver Sir Henry 'Tim' Birkin commissioned Amherst Villiers to design a 'blower' for the existing 4½-litre model, despite protestations from the man behind the name that it would only harm the car's famed reliability. Birkin had the backing of Captain Woolf Barnato, the millionaire racer whose money had saved the marque from liquidation in 1926, so the supercharged version became a production model from 1929 onwards.

Ultimately, the four-cylinder leviathan proved devastatingly quick – it held the lap record at Brooklands for two years – but rarely lasted the distance. The best-ever result would be second overall, behind arch-rival Bugatti, in the 1930 French Grand Prix at Pau. By 1931, after just fifty-five cars had been completed, the receivers had been called in. The 'Blower' Bentley was the last of a dying breed: a proper competition car rather than a conveyance for plutocrats. The winged-B mascot has never sat on anything quite like it since.

Although it was never a great racing car, the 'Blower' Bentley is perhaps the most evocative model the firm has ever produced. Yet marque-founder Walter Owen Bentley hated it.

This example of the Bentley 4½-litre Supercharged was bodied by London firm Vanden Plas, an associate firm of Belgian coachbuilder Van den Plas. Several Bentleys featured similar outlines, although a number have subsequently been converted to more simplistic silhouettes based on those of the stripped-down Le Mans racers.

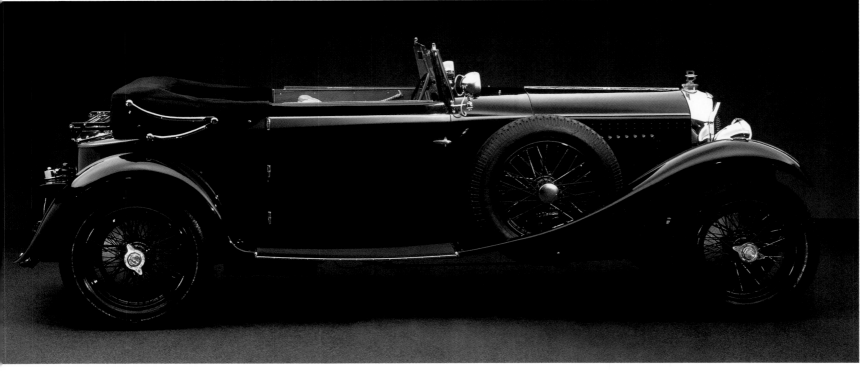

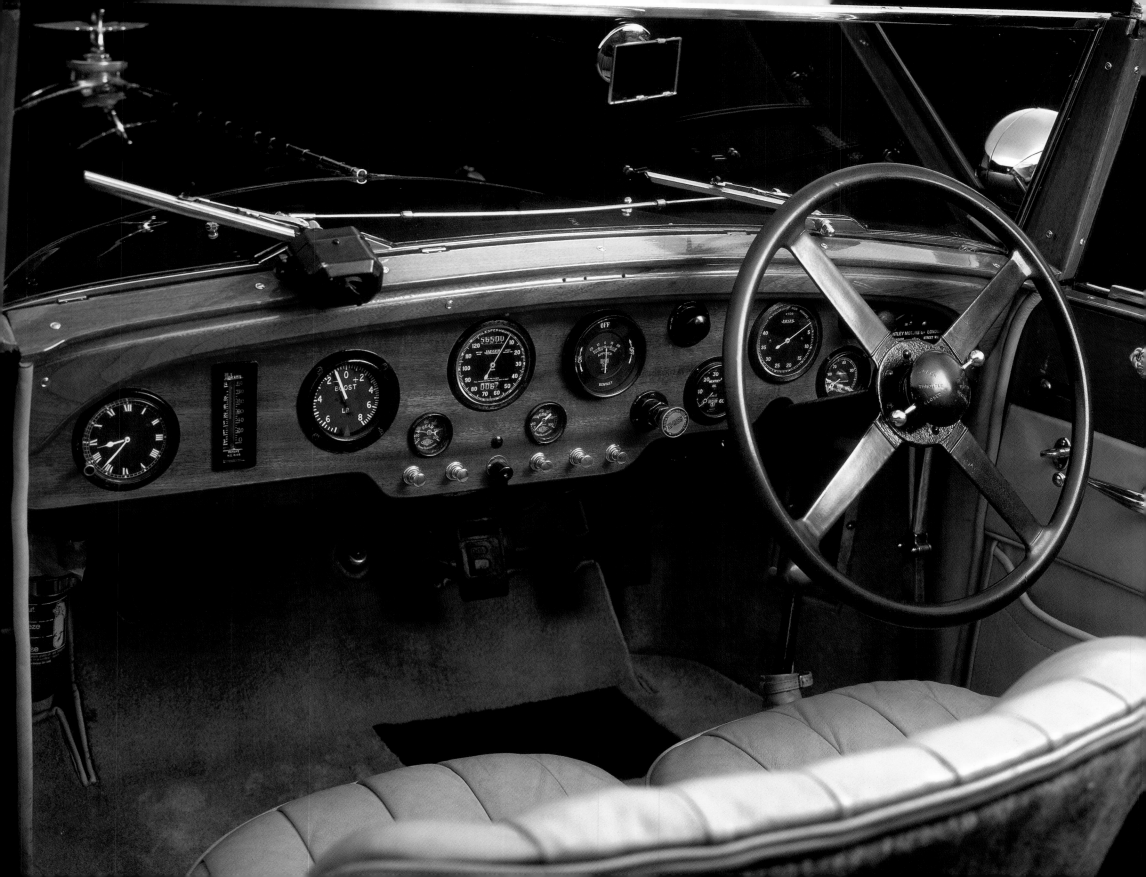

Opposite: Inside, the well-stocked dashboard houses large Jaeger instruments. The gear lever is mounted to the driver's right-hand side. The actual gear change is very heavy but precise.

Right: The 'Blower' Bentley's immensity is not immediately obvious here. The relatively sedate outline only hints at the car's performance capabilities, which were remarkable for their day.

GX 555

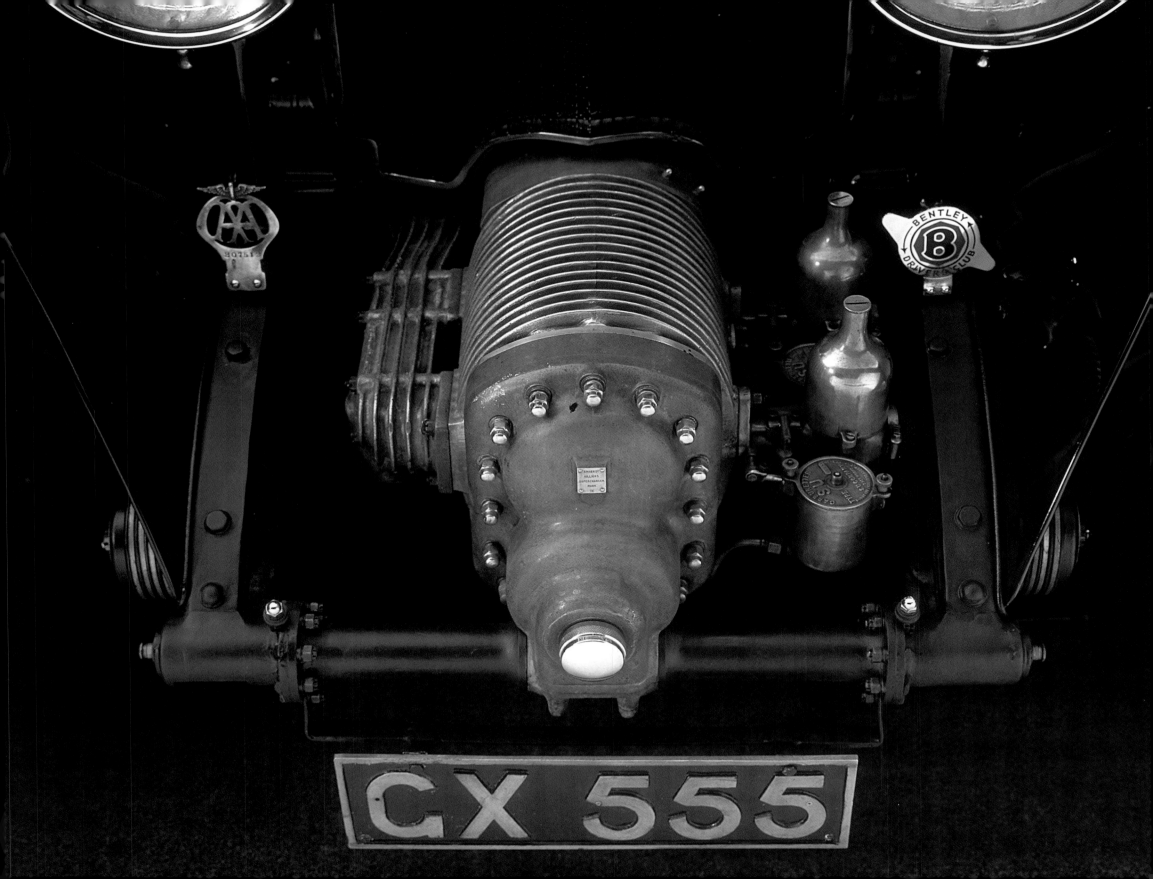

Opposite : The Amherst Villiers-conceived supercharger was financed by millionaire Woolf Barnato, who had saved Bentley from liquidation in 1926. It added power, but 'Blowers' were dogged with unreliability in competition.

Left: The straight-four engine is beautifully finished. Prior to the supercharger conversion, this vast unit had powered the Bentley that won the Le Mans 24 Hour Race in 1928.

1929 GOLDEN ARROW

There has never been a shortage of men willing to risk their lives in the pursuit of new frontiers. During the 1920s and 1930s the world land speed record was a constantly moving target as ever more powerful cars were constructed and new record attempts made. Some resulted in success, others in fatality. Each attempt brought with it fresh challenges as the press and public alike clamoured to see these men push the outer edges of human endeavour.

One man who was not afraid to take such risks was American-born Englishman Major Henry O'Neal de Hane Segrave. Having twice survived being shot during World War I, he took to motor racing and record breaking, vying with that other titan of the period, Sir Malcolm Campbell. The protagonists took it in turn to beat each other's record in a rivalry that started on the long, flat sands of Southport, Lancashire, and reached its zenith at Daytona Beach, Florida.

By 1928 Campbell had pushed his Bluebird to 206 mph (331.5 km/h), but his new record was broken within two months when American Ray Keech recorded 207 mph (333 km/h) in the Triplex Special. Segrave responded with the Golden Arrow. Built at a cost of £11,559, his new challenger was designed by Captain J.S. Irving and powered by a 900-bhp, 23.9-litre Napier Lion 12-cylinder aero engine encased in a radical-looking aluminium body created by coachbuilder Thrupp & Maberly. Although the car was initially called the Irving–Napier Special, its pointed nose and vivid hue swiftly prompted the more evocative name of Golden Arrow.

In front of a vast crowd on 11 March 1929, Segrave made his bid for glory. After two runs down Daytona Beach, his average speed was 231.44 mph (372.4 km/h): the record was his. On his return to England, Segrave was awarded a knighthood and transferred his attentions to breaking records on water. He was killed in June 1930 after his boat, *Miss England II*, hit a log at great speed on Lake Windermere.

The Golden Arrow is perhaps the most beautiful car to have achieved a land speed record. It was designed by J.S. Irving and employed a 23.9-litre aeroplane engine, along with the latest in aerodynamic theory.

Left: Irving sculpted the Golden Arrow around the profile of the engine so tightly that at speed it made a hole in the air not much larger than that of a regular saloon car. Originally the car wore a telescopic sight mounted on the long bonnet, in order to help Segrave aim at the finishing post during his record bid.

Opposite: The car's radical form borrowed ideas from aeronautical design. The underside was designed like an aircraft wing but in reverse, so as to suck itself to the ground – to create downforce – at over 200 mph (320 km/h). This theory of 'ground effect' was reinvented in the 1970s in Formula One racing.

1932 MG K3 MAGNETTE

MG has enjoyed as many hits as misses; marque fans justifiably count the K3 Magnette among its successes. In its time the K3 vanquished rivals in motor sport while handily doubling as a formidable road car. It only adds to its stature that a roll-call of heroes, including Tazio Nuvolari, Richard Seaman, George Eyston, Earl Howe, Whitney Straight and Sir Henry 'Tim' Birkin, used the model to win so many significant races, giving a boost to British motor racing morale when it had been hitherto at a low ebb.

MG's inspirational head, Cecil Kimber, originally conceived a car to fill the gap between the little Midget and the altogether larger Magna models. Something with a displacement of around 1.1 litres would be perfect, and that just happened to be the limit for International Class G, a popular racing class at the time. MG's engineers took the Magna's humdrum straight-six engine and, by lowering its stroke, reduced capacity to 1087 cc. On to this then went a special crossflow cylinder head and magneto ignition. The new strain into which this engine was inserted was dubbed Magnette (or 'little Magna'), and was offered with a choice of wheelbases: 9 ft (2743 mm) for the K1 edition and 7 ft 10³⁄₁₆ in. (2392 mm) for the K2.

One person who was particularly intrigued by the car was Earl Howe. An arch-patriot and accomplished racing driver, he persuaded MG's management to build a competition variant: the K3. A team of three supercharged cars was entered in the 1933 Mille Miglia road race, in which George Eyston led Howe home to take class honours. Later that year the great Italian driver Tazio Nuvolari dominated the Ulster Tourist Trophy in his K3, while MG came close to winning the following year's Le Mans 24 Hour Race before an accident hastened retirement. The K3 – the first car to feature a pre-selector gearbox in competition – was also available to privateers, some later cars featuring single-seater bodywork. MG officially pulled out of motor sport in 1935, by which time thirty-three examples of the car had been made.

With the K3, MG became a major player in international motor sport, attracting a number of high-profile drivers, including the great Tazio Nuvolari. Despite its meagre engine displacement – just 1.1 litres – the six-cylinder machine was always in contention for overall honours as well as class wins.

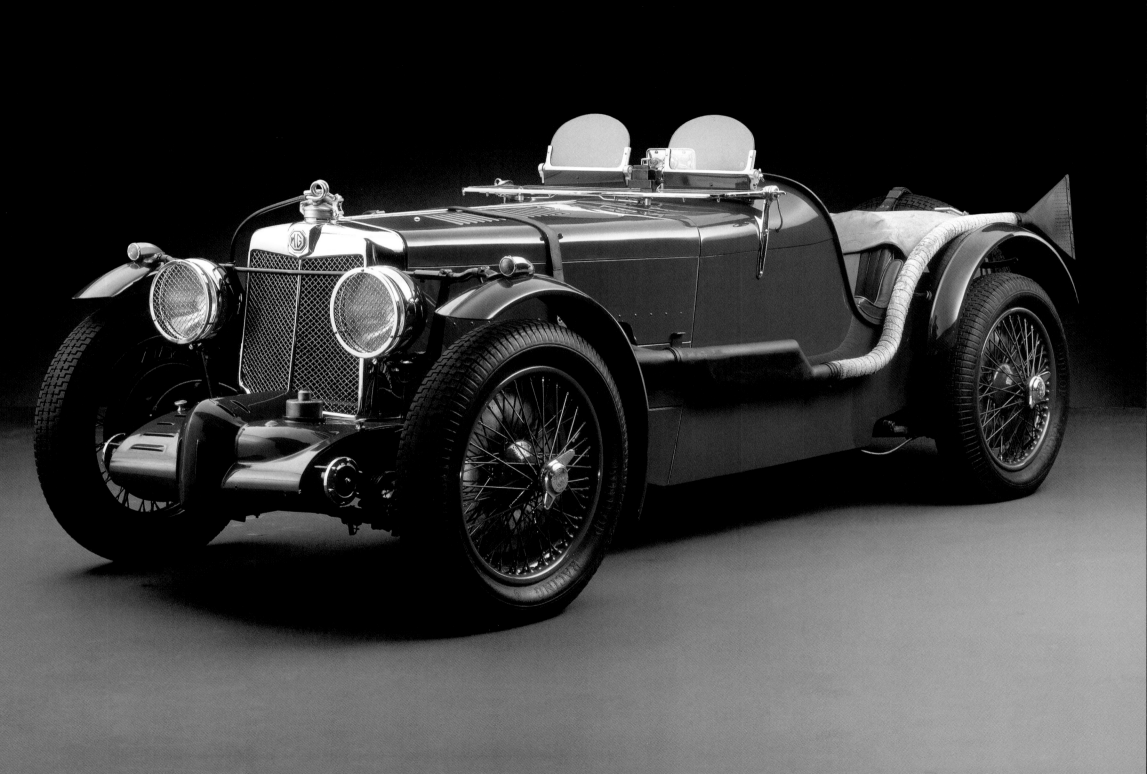

Although no great beauty, the K3 Magnette bore a functional elegance. The square-rigged body was very much in keeping with motor sport-orientated sports cars of the day: all superfluous additions were shed to save weight.

1933 LAGONDA M45

According to the old adage, success comes before a fall. In Lagonda's case, it was the other away around. Among the forgotten Le Mans 24 Hour endurance wins, Lagonda's triumph at the Circuit de la Sarthe in 1935 was all the more remarkable as the marque had lurched into receivership in April of that year, two months before the race. It was in no position to promote the achievement. All this is fairly typical of a marque that technically still exists but, over a century of manufacture, has endured its fair share of fallow years.

The marque was christened by American-born Wilbur Gunn, who named it after a river, Lagonda Creek, that ran through his birthplace of Springfield, Ohio. After a moderately successful career as an opera singer, Gunn arrived in England and began making motorcycles in the greenhouse of his property in Staines, Middlesex. In 1906 the Lagonda Motor Company was formed, initially building three-wheeled 'tricars'. Following Gunn's death in 1920, the firm's directors gradually pushed the brand further upmarket, with the M45 – the largest Lagonda to date – arriving in 1933. It was very much in the spirit of rival Bentleys, but the proprietary 4467-cc Meadows 6ESC straight-six engine was powerful enough to propel the car to 95 mph (153 km/h). Tourer and saloon models were offered, and the altogether racier M45R (Rapide), with a shorter wheelbase and higher state of tune, was introduced in 1935.

Naturally, the M45R soon caught the attention of the motor-racing fraternity, not least Arthur Fox, who acquired three rolling chassis and had them prepared for competition, basing them on a 10 ft 3 in. (3120 mm) wheelbase rather than the standard 10 ft 9 in. (3270 mm). An extensive dieting regime ensured a weight of 3359 lb (1524 kg) with 27 gallons/122 litres of fuel, a saving of 271 lb (123 kg) over the production car. When two of these M45s were entered for the 1935 Le Mans race, Dr J.D. Benjafield and Sir Ronald Gunter took the flag in one, with the sister car in thirteenth place.

The M45 was upright, rectilinear and handsome; this example's two-door configuration hints at the marque's sporting credentials. In 1935 Lagonda won the Le Mans 24 Hour endurance race. Unfortunately, the firm was in no place to capitalize on this success, as bankruptcy loomed.

There was nothing especially radical in the M45's make-up, with its Bentley-esque sense of scale, although the use of proprietary Meadows engines meant that it perhaps wasn't as pure-bred as its more exalted rival.

1933 NAPIER-RAILTON

Enigmatic, taciturn and not one to suffer fools gladly or otherwise, John Rhodes Cobb was a man who was greatly respected for his achievements but often treated with wariness. He accumulated wealth in the fur trade, and an interest in fast cars inevitably led to motor sport; he won his first event in 1925 aboard a 10-litre Fiat. Bigger, faster machines followed, culminating in what, to many, remains the ultimate pre-war racing car: the Napier-Railton.

Designed by Reid Railton and created in the Thomson & Taylor workshops at Brooklands, Surrey, in 1933, this monstrous device featured a 12-cylinder, 24-litre Napier Lion aero engine allied to a three-speed transmission, all housed in an immensely strong girder frame. Although it was capable of reaching 168 mph (270 km/h), braking was to the rear wheels only, a terrifying concept since the car was primarily raced on the steeply banked – and heavily rutted – Brooklands circuit. Period images show all four wheels off the ground as Cobb thundered to victory.

As holder of both the standing start and flying start lap records, and as winner of the fastest long-distance race ever run at Brooklands, Cobb vanquished all comers in the Napier-Railton. His Outer Circuit lap record of 143.4 mph (230.7 km/h) remained unbroken when the Surrey track fell silent in 1939.

Cobb subsequently turned his attention to the land speed record. In 1938 he drove the futuristic, twin Napier-engined Mobil Railton to 350.2 mph (563.5 km/h) on the Utah salt flats to become the fastest man on earth. In 1947 he raised it to 394.1 mph (634.2 km/h). He lost his life five years later when the jet boat he was driving disintegrated at high speed on Loch Ness.

The fastest car ever to have stormed the famous Brooklands circuit, the Napier-Railton was a record-breaking monster. In the 1960s it was still a challenger for overall honours in Formula Libre races, in the hands of the Hon. Patrick Lindsay.

With a 24-litre engine allied to a three-speed gearbox — and with rear braking only — the Napier-Railton was a formidable and intimidating machine. It was built by Thomson & Taylor and was reputedly capable of 168 mph (270 km/h) flat out.

The Napier-Railton is
starkly efficient and its
form follows its function
(racing), yet there's a certain
brutal elegance to its lines.
The vast steering wheel
gave John Cobb something
to cling on to as he blasted
over the bumps at the
Brooklands circuit in the
days before seat belts.
In 1951 the car appeared in
the film *Pandora and the
Flying Dutchman*, which
starred James Mason.

Left: The Napier-Railton's monstrous 12-cylinder engine has a maximum revs of just 3000 rpm. With a 65-gallon (295-litre) fuel tank, it did at best 5 mpg (56.5 l/100 km) and took ten minutes to refuel.

Opposite: Heavy engineering of the Napier-Railton's steering and suspension components added much-needed durability in long-distance races.

1934   ERA

English Racing Automobiles (ERA) was founded in late 1933 by Humphrey Cook with the single aim of taking on the might of Italian and German manufacturers at international-level motor sport. But it was largely thanks to the backing and enthusiasm of flamboyant and wealthy driver Raymond Mays, and the technical expertise of self-trained engineer Peter Berthon, that the project reached fruition.

Mays had campaigned Bugattis, ACs and a supercharged Vauxhall before a successful season in 1933 aboard a Berthon-prepared 1.5-litre Riley (known universally as the White Riley). This effectively became the prototype ERA. Mays's family were Lincolnshire grain merchants, and it was on a substantial property in Bourne that the ERA factory was based.

Plans called for a car to compete in the 'Voiturette' class (up to 1.5 litres), with the production racer – the car shown here being the very first – featuring a chassis designed in part by Reid Railton. Its six-cylinder engine was nearly identical to that of the White Riley, with twin camshafts mounted either side of the cylinder block and a Murray Jamieson-conceived supercharger. It ran on methanol, and power was transmitted to the rear wheels via a four-speed pre-selector Wilson transmission. The car produced around 150 bhp at 6500 rpm in 1.5-litre trim, and 1.1-litre and 2-litre versions were also offered. They were priced at £1500, and seventeen were sold, to customers who included such stars of the period as the racing driver Richard Seaman and Prince Bira of Siam. Although never a match for the mighty (and infinitely better financed) Auto Unions or Mercedes-Benz racers, ERAs were continuously developed prior to World War II and remained competitive enough for Mays to win the 1947–48 British Hillclimb championships.

In 1948 the company was acquired by Leslie Johnson, who initiated the Bristol-powered G-type, but the project was later abandoned. Aside from a sports-car design that ultimately led to the Jowett Javelin, the ERA name remained dormant until the late 1980s, when it was ignominiously applied to turbo-charged Minis and Skodas.

Thanks to English Racing Automobiles, Great Britain had a challenger to Continental fare from the likes of Alfa Romeo and Maserati. Although ERA was not really in the fight for Grand Prix honours, it was competitive at national level and in 'Voiturette' races.

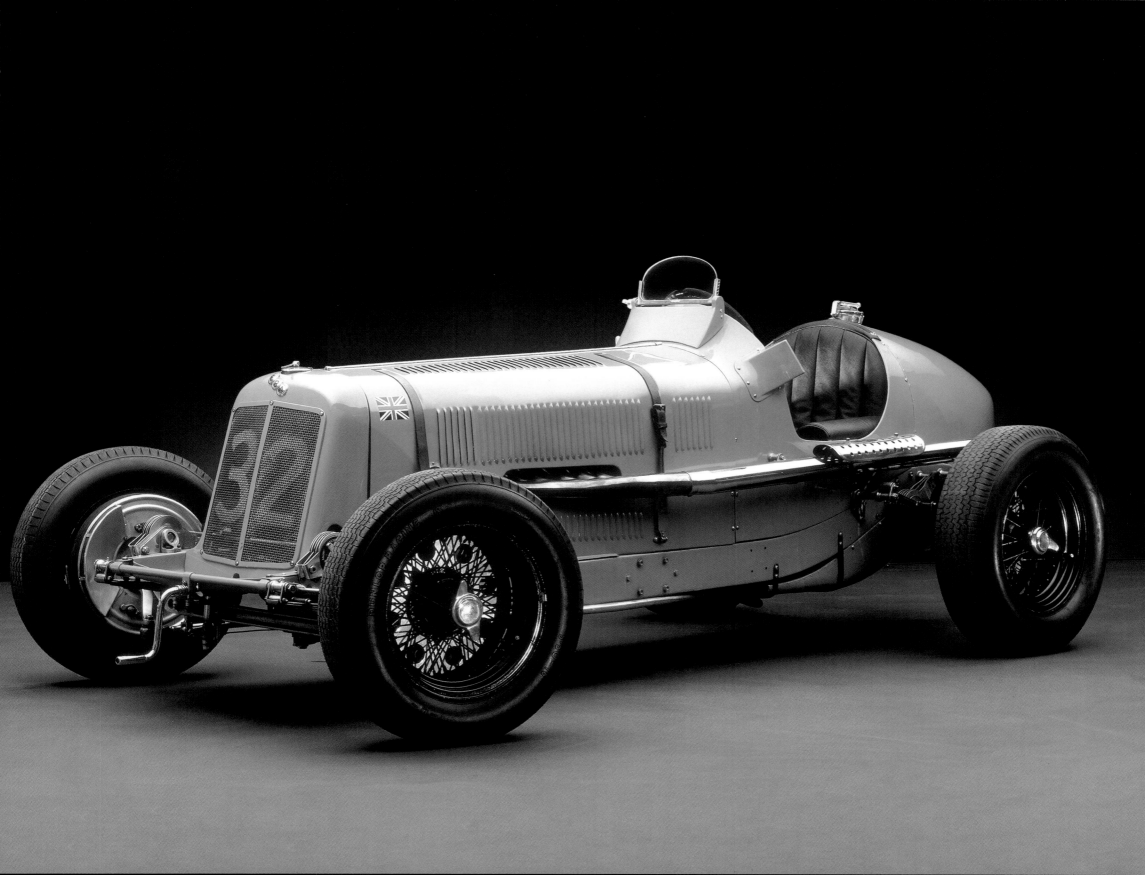

ERA is much more than just another
long-departed racing marque, and its
cars have never strayed far from the
circuits, continuing to entertain crowds
at historic events. They command a
loyal retinue, most owners retaining
them for decades.

Left: The dropped axle beam had holes drilled into it in order to save weight. Drum brakes endowed this car with the ability to out-brake opponents.

Opposite: The ERA's supercharged engine was derived from a Riley unit, with twin camshafts mounted high on either side of the cylinder block. ERAs originally ran on methanol fuel and drove through a four-speed epicyclical gearbox.

1935 HRG 1500

When the triumvirate of Ted Halford, Guy Robins and H.R. Godfrey pooled the first letters of their respective surnames and produced the first HRG in October 1935, their offspring was already obsolete. Its technology owed more to the previous decade: a rugged chassis comprising two parallel C-section channels running fore and aft, strengthened by tubular cross-members, the front beam axle stuck far out in front, supported by quarter-elliptic springs and located by the arms of friction shock absorbers. With semi-elliptic springs at the back, there wasn't much in the way of elasticity to keep all four wheels in contact with the road, the ash frame beneath the skimpy but attractive body being designed to flex. Yet HRGs handled well, and these 1.5-litre Meadows-powered machines soon proved effective in competition. One example, driven by Marcus Chambers and Peter Clark, won its class in the Le Mans 24 Hour Race in 1939, a year after 1.1- or 1.5-litre Singer-derived engines had been substituted.

When the marque returned after the war, a significantly different HRG hit the market alongside the traditional 1100 and 1500 models. Gone was the square-rigged, perpendicular body, to be replaced by a radical full-width silhouette that lived up to its Aerodynamic nomenclature. Unfortunately, this new strain had one fairly fundamental flaw: beneath the skin was essentially the same basic structure as before, and the aluminium coachwork wasn't up to the task of countering the flexing.

Nonetheless, HRG continued to be successful in motor sport. In 1949 Eric Thompson and Jack Fairman drove a specially bodied 1500 (christened the 'Mobile Galosh') to an astonishing eighth overall and class honours at Le Mans. Having survived one round-the-clock classic, the duo headed for the Spa circuit in Belgium to tackle another. The result was two class wins in as many weekends. HRG lived on until 1966, making cars in small numbers. Survivors continue to provide great entertainment for their owners.

Rudimentary and unsophisticated they may be, yet HRGs are nevertheless hugely entertaining to drive, and much more than the sum of their proprietary parts.

1935 SS100 JAGUAR

Bill (later Sir William) Lyons had an exceptional eye for detail. He was never a great innovator, but was blessed with an innate ability when it came to distilling and refining influences into a perfectly proportioned whole. He understood his art, even if his draughtsmanship was poor; he knew what was right and what worked. Although his first sports cars were viewed with disdain by some at the time for their use of proprietary running gear, they served their purpose in promoting his company's sporting pretensions.

The SS90, introduced in 1935, was based on a shortened chassis borrowed from the contemporary SS1 saloon and featured a 2663-cc straight-six Standard engine. Just twenty-three were built before it was replaced by the SS100. Outwardly identifiable by its larger headlights and inclined fuel tank, the SS100 featured beneath the rakish exterior a redesigned overhead valve cylinder head and SU carburettors that increased power from 70 bhp to 104 bhp. *The Autocar* magazine tested the factory demonstrator and recorded a top speed of 95 mph (153 km/h) and a 0–60 mph (100 km/h) time of 13.5 seconds. In 1937 Jaguar offered a larger displacement 3485-cc engine, which produced a healthy 125 bhp, enough to propel the car past the magic 100 mph (160 km/h) mark. As Jaguar took its first faltering steps into motor-sport legend, early victories for the marque included the 1936 Alpine Rally and the following year's RAC Rally.

Where the SS series really scored was in value for money. The Jaguar maxim of 'grace, space and pace' was certainly true, but its cars were offered at a knock-down price. In 1937 a 2.5-litre cost £395, easily undercutting its rivals. Yet while the SS100 is considered to be one of the most aesthetically accomplished of all Jaguar models, it is also one of the rarest, with just 314 of all kinds being made up to 1939.

Nowadays the SS100 is considered to be among the prettiest of all pre-war sports cars, but when it was first produced it was derided for being too flash.

With screen and hood in place, the
SS100 loses much of its elegance, but
the same applies to most cars of the day.
With the windshield folded down, the
rakish splendour of the SS100 is all too
obvious. It really is a beautiful machine,
and belies the humble ancestry of its
proprietary Standard running gear.

1936 ALVIS SPEED 25

The Alvis name still exists, but the last car to bear the distinctive red triangle badge left the company's once-famous factory in Holyhead Road, Coventry, in 1967: a foreseeable outcome to a decision made more than thirty years earlier. Founded in 1920 by entrepreneurial Welshman Thomas George John, the firm prevailed when so many rivals succumbed during the Depression years, but only by diversifying. In 1933 Alvis bought manufacturing rights to French Gnome-Rhône radial aero engines, a move that ensured the company's long-term survival but, ultimately, at the expense of car manufacturing.

This was a minor tragedy, as Alvis was once among the most forward-thinking quality marques, pioneering front-wheel drive, servo-assisted brakes and synchromesh gearboxes. Conceived, if only in part, by Captain G.T. Smith-Clarke, George Lanchester and Harry Mundy (later the architect of near-legendary Coventry Climax and Jaguar engines), the Speed 25 was closely related to the 4.3-litre Alvis. Both models were introduced in 1936 and shared a seven-bearing straight-six engine that differed between models in displacement (3571 cc and 4387 cc respectively). The former featured triple SU carburettors and was good for 106 bhp at 3800 rpm and a top speed of 95 mph (153 km/h). It also had the distinction of being the first Alvis to feature an accelerator on the right-hand side of the brake pedal as opposed to the left. As with so many luxury marques of the day, Alvis employed outside coachbuilders to clothe its products (it didn't possess a body shop), with Cross & Ellis, Charlesworth and Mulliner being among favoured couturiers. Around four hundred cars were made in saloon and convertible form.

By the outbreak of World War II, car production had dwindled to nothing, although a contract to assemble Rolls-Royce Kestrel, Merlin and Griffon aeroplane engines ensured that Alvis came out of the conflict in a far healthier state than when it entered. The name is currently applied to all manner of military vehicles.

The dramatic outline on this Speed 25 was created by London-based coachbuilder Lancefield for the 1938 London Motor Show.

Opposite: For the 'Concealed Drophead Coupé', Lancefield cribbed its earlier efforts on a Mercedes-Benz 540K chassis, including the fluted waistline and wheel spats.

Right: The rear-hinged doors allow access to a sumptuously trimmed cabin, in which rear passengers are afforded plenty of legroom.

1945 MG TC MIDGET

Although the TC was essentially a recycled pre-war model, its importance to MG's history – and to that of the British motor industry as a whole – cannot be overestimated. It was responsible for introducing the concept of the sports car to the USA and, in doing so, opened the floodgates for later models and other marques to trail in its wake. Following the TC's arrival Stateside, MG became a generic term for a sports car, if only briefly. When asked what MG stood for, owners would routinely answer: 'mighty good'.

The TC, introduced in 1945, was similar in make-up to the pre-war TB, sharing the same 45-bhp, 1250-cc XPAG four-cylinder engine (with a slightly higher compression ratio), but with a wider cabin that was right-hand-drive only. Performance was never electrifying: 0–60 mph (100 km/h) took a leisurely 22.7 seconds and top speed was a mere 77 mph (124 km/h), but this was at a time when the average British saloon would struggle to better 60 mph (97 km/h). The chassis flexed, as did the scuttle, while the beam axle lent it a fillings-loosening ride quality. Even so, drivers fell in love with the TC's cheeky character and an outline that was left to evolve rather than actually styled: the slab sides, cutaway doors and separate wings remained a constant through the T-series range to 1955.

The TC's influence on the American market was out of all proportion to the numbers made. Of the 10,002 believed to have been sold up to 1949, only 2001 went to North America, and it was only in the car's final year of manufacture that MG had an official presence there. Having established a bridgehead in the USA, MG then built 29,664 of the following model, the TD, in four years, with 90 per cent being for export markets.

The diminutive TC helped establish MG as a global player, and introduced North America to the concept of the sports car.

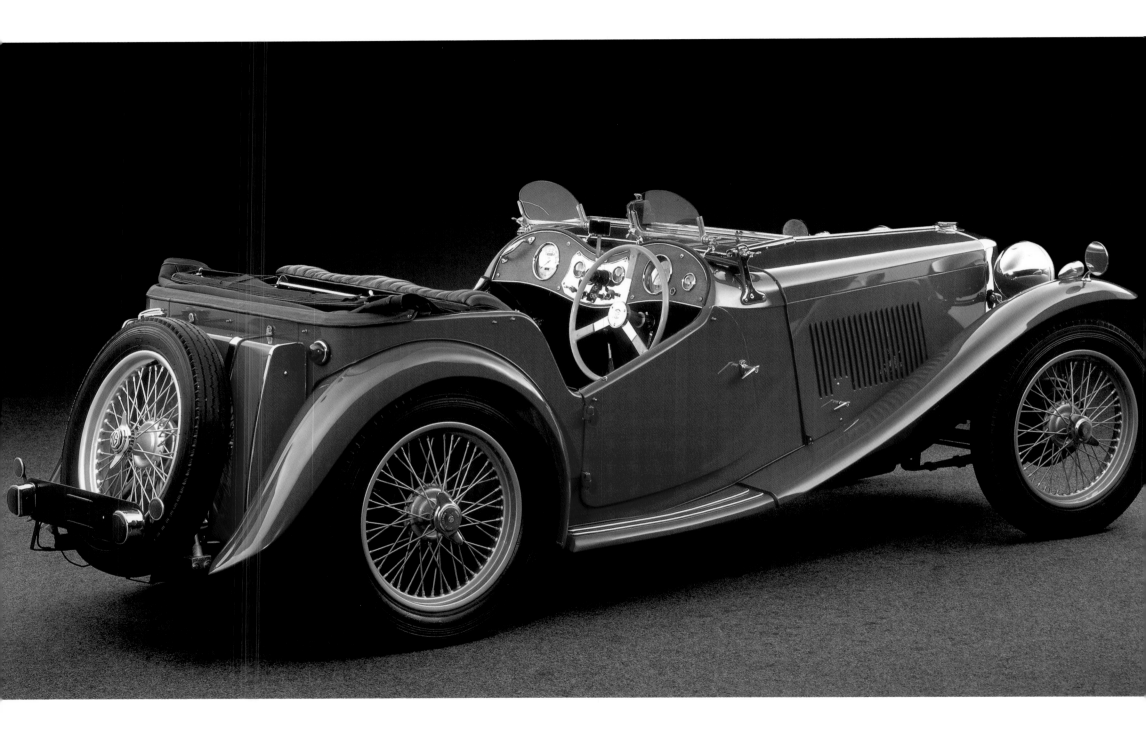

Rakish styling (opposite) harked back to the pre-war era. A shapely dashboard (right) housed minimal instrumentation; in keeping with the model's stark manifesto, there was no more information than was strictly necessary.

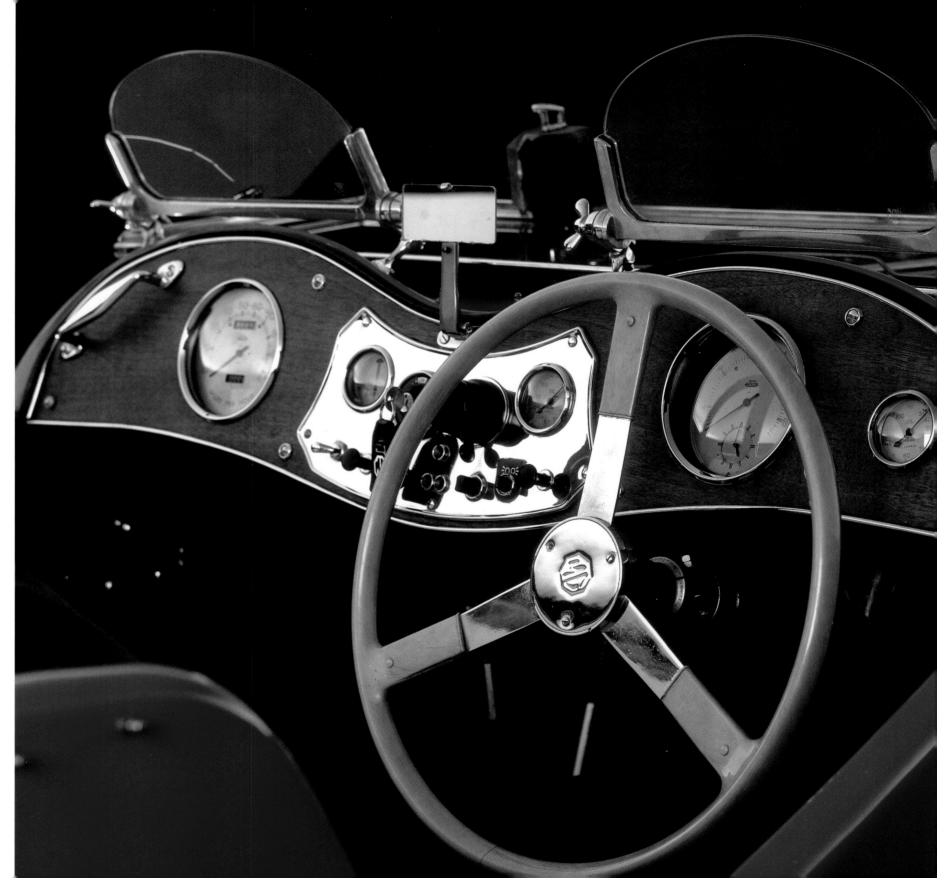

Opposite: The perpendicular radiator grille was a familiar MG styling trait dating back to the 1930s. The windscreen could fold flat if the driver wanted to feel the full force of the airflow.

Right: The TC's narrow track is especially evident here. Spindly tyres and a flexible chassis made for a lively driving experience, but the car's handling was remarkably good for the period.

1946 TRIUMPH 1800/2000 ROADSTER

The Roadster was designed at the tail end of World War II, shortly before Triumph was bought out by the Standard Motor Company in December 1945. The firm's maverick managing director, Sir John Black (known to some as the Black Knight), wanted a sports car to tackle its Jaguar rival, which had made use of Standard engines during the 1930s. The Roadster's styling is attributed to Frank Callaby and Arthur Ballard. Forty years on, the car became ingrained in British popular culture through its starring role in the BBC's *Bergerac* TV series of the 1980s.

Owing to steel shortages just after World War II, the 1800's body was constructed from aluminium (with steel front wings). The tubular cross-braced chassis featured transverse leaf-sprung independent front suspension with a live axle and half-elliptic springs at the rear. Power came from a 1776-cc overhead valve four-cylinder engine allied to a four-speed gearbox with a column-mounted lever.

This largely handmade car was beautifully appointed, although visually outmoded, with its large separate headlights and near-vertical radiator grille. Triumph claimed it was a three-seater thanks to the use of a bench seat, with additional room for two provided at the rear where the boot housed a 'dicky seat'. It was far from sporting, though: in 1947 *The Autocar* recorded a top speed of 75 mph (120 km/h) and a 0–60 mph (100 km/h) time of a glacial 34.4 seconds.

In 1948 the 1800 was succeeded by the 2000 Roadster, which featured a longer chassis made of pressed steel and a 2008-cc Standard Vanguard engine. Front suspension was now by means of coil springs and double wishbones. Top speed was marginally increased to 77 mph (124 km/h), the 0–60 mph (100 km/h) sprint being shaved to 27.9 seconds. Launched at that year's London Motor Show, where the Jaguar XK120 (see p. 111) also made its maiden bow, the Triumph suddenly looked even more out of touch and was dropped a year later. Around 4500 of both types were made.

It was archaic and a touch dumpy, perhaps, but the Roadster marked the beginning of Triumph's post-war ascent to sports-car greatness. Pictured here is a 2000 Roadster.

1947 BRISTOL 400

Bristol has always been distinct from other marques, being seemingly impervious to changes in fashion and fickle market share. A major manufacturer probably builds more cars in an hour than Bristol has managed in sixty years: it is simply a small but glorious sliver of British motoring heritage, albeit one that has German genes.

Having hitherto been a key player in the aero industry, building complete airframes as well as engines, Bristol's arrival as a car maker was hastened by the end of World War II, when the firm found itself with spare manufacturing capacity. The decision was made to build a high-quality car that would mirror the company's commanding image in the skies. Rather than starting from scratch, however, Bristol's engineers looked to one of the best pre-war cars as inspiration: the BMW 327. An ally was found in H.J. Aldington, who had imported the German cars under the Frazer Nash banner during the 1930s. With his assistance, and under the guise of war reparations, Bristol not only gained detailed plans of BMW engines and chassis, but also landed highly respected engineer Dr Fritz Fiedler as an adviser.

When introduced at the Geneva Salon in March 1947, the Bristol 400 looked not unlike an anglicized BMW, right down to the familiar kidney-shaped grilles. Its chassis was bang up to date, employing independent, transverse leaf front suspension and rear longitudinal torsion bars linked to double-acting shock absorbers made in-house. Power came from a 1971-cc six-cylinder single-camshaft engine that, even in a moderate state of tune, produced around 80 bhp. This unit proved its worth on numerous motor-racing tracks, and powered subsequent models until 1963. Despite a hefty price tag of £2724, the 400 remained in production for three years. It was replaced by the 401, which married Alfa Romeo-inspired styling and aerodynamic excellence in one enticing package.

Borrowing heavily from its aeronautical background, Bristol created a highly advanced outline for its first automobile. The 400's straight-six engine was greatly influenced by German technology.

LEA-FRANCIS 14HP/18HP

As with so many Coventry-based car manufacturers, Lea-Francis's origins were in two-wheeled vehicles. Richard H. Lea and Graham I. Francis built their first bicycle in 1895, turning to automobiles eight years later with a strange vehicle that featured a three-cylinder engine mounted transversely under its floor. The marque went on to find success in motor sport, but its often precarious financial state prevented it from taking on the bigger players.

Lea-Francis did, however, emerge suitably fortified from World War II, having earned substantial profits as an engineering subcontractor. With funds in place, the firm launched its range of post-war cars in 1946. The 14HP – powered by a 1776-cc straight-six engine – was offered in saloon-car form with bodies by AP Aircraft, although bare chassis were offered to other coachbuilders. Many of these were built up as estate cars to take advantage of tax breaks: so-called 'shooting brakes' were classed as commercial vehicles and so were exempt from purchase tax.

In 1947 the range was augmented with a new sports-car variant. The 14HP featured a twin-carburettor engine tuned to produce 85 bhp, but a larger-capacity model, 2496 cc and 18HP, arrived in 1949. With 105 bhp, this pretty roadster could top 100 mph (160 km/h). Other developments that year included the adoption of torsion bar independent front suspension in place of leaf springs.

Unfortunately, manufacturing cars in small runs was never profitable, and the last chassis was made in 1952 (although cars were still being sold in 1954). Since then there have been numerous attempts at a Lea-Francis revival. The hideous Lynx, which first appeared at the 1960 London Motor Show, proved a dismal flop, with just three cars being made. A further attempt two years later with an upmarket saloon dubbed Crusader ended before the prototype was finished. Most recently, an all-new sports car, the 30/230 (for 3.0 litres/230 km/h), designed by ex-Jaguar man Jim Randle, broke cover at the 1998 Birmingham Motor Show but has so far failed to reach production.

Although forgotten in recent years, Lea-Francis once had a proud sporting heritage. The 14HP/18HP models continued the trend in the years immediately after World War II.

Opposite: The straight-six engine was admired in its day for its power output, some examples being used for motor-sport applications, most memorably by racing-car manufacturer Connaught.

Below: Although they were of no great beauty – no Lea-Francis ever was – the 14HP/18HP's swept-back lines were very much of the period and displayed sporting intent.

1948 JAGUAR XK120

By the end of World War II, Jaguar Cars needed a fresh model to replace the SS100 (see p. 89). Plans to build a new 2-litre, four-cylinder sports car were dropped on grounds of cost, while the MkVII saloon was still in the prototype stage. In an effort to drum up interest in the marque in general and the forthcoming 3.4-litre, twin-cam straight-six engine in particular, company principal William Lyons exhibited the XK Open Two-Seater Super Sports at the 1948 London Motor Show. It was effectively a concept car, a test bed. There were no firm plans for it ever to enter production, but such was the overwhelming response that Lyons was left with little choice.

Swiftly renamed the XK120 – X for experimental, K the sequence of engine design and 120 mph (193 km/h) its projected top speed – the initial batch of 239 cars featured handcrafted aluminium bodies and laminated ash frames. Lyons deemed it a low-volume product, almost a distraction, but with a launch price of £998 it represented remarkable value for money, so demand soon outstripped supply. Coachbuilding techniques were no longer sufficient: from 1950 a fully fledged production version was initiated, featuring a pressed-steel hull with alloy doors, bonnet and boot lid. The first model became known as the XK120 Roadster following the introduction in 1951 of the Fixed-Head Coupé, which in turn was followed two years later by the Drophead Coupé Cabriolet.

Although the SS100 had enjoyed competition success, it was the XK120 that truly established Jaguar as a serious player in motor sport. Ian Appleyard, Lyons's son-in-law, scored a hat-trick of victories for the model on the Alpine Rally from 1950 to 1952, also winning the RAC and Tulip rallies in 1951. In August 1952 Stirling Moss, Jack Fairman, Leslie Johnson and Bert Hadley pounded the Linas-Montlhéry circuit, near Paris, for seven days and seven nights in an XK120 coupé: they averaged 100 mph (160 km/h) for 168 hours and broke eight world records in the process. After five years in production, by which time 12,078 had been made, the XK120 made way for the XK140, its legendary status assured.

The XK120 caused a sensation when it first appeared in 1948. The styling borrowed cues from a pre-war competition-bred BMW but was infinitely prettier. The straight-six XK engine would remain in production until the 1990s.

Styled, if only in part, by marque boss William Lyons, the XK had a perfectly proportioned outline that was mirrored by its mechanical beauty. The split-V windscreen was an idea borrowed from contemporary speedboats.

With the XK120, Jaguar became a marque in its own right rather than a model designation. It set the template for generations of future models: beauty, pace and affordability. There is no denying, however, that the car's cabin (opposite) was cramped and the ride quality poor.

1950 ASTON MARTIN DB2

Having acquired Aston Martin in 1947, tractor magnate David Brown set about breathing life into the beleaguered marque. He did so by purchasing the equally cash-strapped Lagonda, principally to obtain rights to its new 2.6-litre straight-six engine, which had been designed by Willie Wilson under guidance from the great W.O. Bentley. The addition of a Claude Hill-designed tubular chassis, clothed in an elegant aluminium body styled by Frank Feeley, resulted in the fabulous DB2.

First shown at the New York Motor Show in April 1950, this sublime GT was an instant hit, even more so after it displayed tremendous promise trackside. That same year George Abecassis and Lance Macklin drove a factory-entered DB2 to an impressive fifth overall in the Le Mans 24 Hour Race, and shared the Index of Performance award. A year on, a lighter car with a 125-bhp Vantage engine (an option from 1951) came third overall and took class honours, courtesy of Macklin and Eric Thompson. This was an extraordinary achievement for what was essentially a road-going production car up against purpose-built machinery. In 1952 a DB2 finished twelfth overall and won its class on the gruelling Mille Miglia, a road race that usually served to highlight a car's weaknesses; it repeated the feat in 1953. By this time, the works team was concentrating on the DB3 racer, and the DB2 was stood down as Aston's front-line weapon of choice.

A total of 411 DB2s are believed to have been made until 1953, including 112 convertibles. The DB2 was replaced by the 2/4, which was more a sophisticated road car than a competition tool.

Arguably the best-looking coupé of its era, the DB2 was British from end to end, its styling the work of unheralded design ace Frank Feeley.

The DB2's balanced outline served as the basis for several further iterations, but none matched the artistry of the original.

1951 JAGUAR C-TYPE

When Peter Walker and Peter Whitehead steered their C-type to victory in the 1951 Le Mans 24 Hour Race at record speed, they at a stroke established Jaguar as a major presence in motor sport. This win on the car's maiden outing laid the foundations for a series of wins at the Circuit de la Sarthe over the course of the decade. Being a Jaguar, the outright competition car was also a 'catalogue model'.

Jaguar had raced the XK120 (see p. 111) in the endurance event a year earlier, but it hadn't been quick enough for outright honours. It also proved fragile in road races, hence the arrival of the XK120C (or C-type). With its lightweight, multi-tubular frame and aluminium body, the new model weighed considerably less than its sibling, although it retained the twin-cam, straight-six engine, tuned to 210 bhp. Front suspension was by means of double wishbones and torsion bars, with a live rear axle carried by twin trailing arms, torsion bars and a Panhard rod. Clothing the ensemble was a curvaceous, fully enveloped body designed by former Bristol aerodynamicist Malcolm Sayer.

Jaguar returned to Le Mans in 1952, but, fearing competition from Mercedes-Benz, substantially altered the car's outline in an effort to gain greater straight-line speed. The new shape necessitated repositioning the cooling system; when all three team cars had to retire because of overheating Jaguar swiftly returned to the more conventional silhouette, suitably chastened. A year on, Duncan Hamilton and Tony Rolt scored an emphatic win at Le Mans, the first ever at an average speed of over 100 mph (160 km/h). In 1954 the C-type bowed out with fourth place for the privateer Ecurie Francorchamps entry driven by Jacques Swaters and Roger Laurent. Fifty-three C-types were made until 1953, and surviving examples regularly attract seven-figure prices.

The C-type won the gruelling Le Mans 24 Hour Race first time out in 1951, and at a stroke Jaguar entered into sporting legend.

Aerodynamicist Malcolm Sayer applied all he had learned in the aviation industry to the Jaguar C-type, his first racing-car design. In doing so, he created a work of art. There are no smart touches or styling tricks, just a pure outline created with the singular purpose of streamlined efficiency.

Left: The Jaguar C-type cabin was typically sparse, offering a near-perpendicular driving position: there were few concessions to comfort.

Opposite: The exhaust pipes emitted from the side of the car in order to avoid the grounding problems that were experienced when they were mounted beneath the car.

Below: Despite being bred with competition in mind, the C-type was entirely usable as a road car. In fact, Jaguar offered it as a 'catalogue model', and many private owners campaigned the C-type with success, driving to and from races.

Opposite: The one-piece flip-forward bonnet reveals the classic XK straight-six engine, itself an object of beauty; it went on to power future generations of competition Jaguars.

1952 · BENTLEY R-TYPE CONTINENTAL

It was simply the finest car of its day, a monument to coachbuilding artistry and a timely reminder of a once-proud sporting lineage. Following the Continental's arrival at the 1952 London Motor Show, Bentley once again had a true high-performance car on its stocks, something that had noticeably been lacking since Rolls-Royce assumed control of the marque in 1931. But for the firm's chief project engineer, Ivan Everden, it might well not have happened at all, as a sceptical board of directors saw no future for a high-performance coupé.

In 1950 Everden first laid out his plans for a luxurious grand tourer that could hit more than 100 mph (160 km/h), originally to have been called Corniche II. Based on the existing R-type saloon chassis, complete with 4.6-litre straight-six engine, the resultant Continental was the fastest four-seater car in the world – and the most expensive. With a launch price of £7600, it was only ever going to tempt the super-rich. And much of its desirability, then and now, can be attributed to the unsung artisans of H.J. Mulliner & Co., who created an outline that cherry-picked the best American and Italian styling cues and imbued them with a distinctive British flavour. That they managed to create such balanced lines on such a large canvas is extraordinary. Equally remarkable is that the aluminium coachwork weighed just 750 lb (340 kg) in its entirety. The relatively streamlined silhouette, honed in Rolls-Royce's wind tunnel, allied to 172 bhp (in the 4.9-litre form), ensured a top speed of a then-staggering 118 mph (190 km/h). As *The Autocar* succinctly reported: 'It brings Bentley back to the forefront of the world's fastest cars.'

In total, 208 R-type Continentals were made, all but fifteen wearing this outline. The rest were clothed by Graber and Franay, with a singleton car being bodied by Pininfarina.

With the launch of the R-type Continental, Bentley revived its sporting intent. Capable of exceeding 100 mph (160 km/h) in utter civility, the Continental was arguably the finest car of its day.

Below: Stylists at coachbuilder H.J. Mulliner & Co. were responsible for the Continental's graceful outline, the nose featuring the familiar Bentley grille but set in a startlingly modern silhouette. The rear view (below right) displays certain aspects borrowed from the Italian Cisitalia 202 and contemporary Cadillac and Oldsmobile designs.

Opposite: In 4.9-litre form, the R-type's straight-six engine produced 172 bhp. That the engine was barely audible whether idling or at cruising speeds is a testimony to the team of engineers that created it under the guidance of Ivan Everden. The car was conceived by him, and entered production despite a sceptical board of directors.

1953 AC ACE

During its rollercoaster existence, AC was never celebrated for breaking moulds or pushing envelopes. It built invalid carriages, rolling stock and just about anything else that could be fabricated. Manufacturing cars was a sideline for the Hurlock family, who took control of the marque in 1930. Yet while production of the Ace never ran into four figures during its nine-year existence, it proved to be one of the most innovative sports cars of its era and paved the way for ever more extreme variations on the theme.

The car's Italianate styling was cribbed directly from the Ferrari 166, the Ace being derived from a one-off racing car commissioned by accomplished driver Cliff Davis and designed by John Tojeiro. This Portuguese-born, English-raised engineer was based in Buntingford, Hertfordshire, where he shared a workshop with Ernie Bailey, who made bodies for AC's dumpy Buckland model. Davis's vigorous campaign of 1953 emphatically proved the design, and, knowing that AC was looking for a new model, Bailey hastened a meeting between all parties. A deal was quickly inked: AC would build a refined iteration as the Ace, with Tojeiro receiving a £5 royalty for every car sold.

When it made its debut at the London Motor Show at the end of 1953, the production Ace employed independent suspension at each end at a time when most cars made do with a live rear axle. AC's aged 2-litre straight-six engine – which could trace its origins back to 1911 – was standard equipment and in ultimate 102-bhp trim meant a top speed of 103 mph (166 km/h) and 0–60 mph (100 km/h) in 11.4 seconds.

In the spring of 1957 AC substituted a BMW-derived Bristol engine that weighed 25 lb (11.3 kg) less than the outgoing version, but was more powerful and revved higher. Performance was enhanced, top speed being upped to 115 mph (185 km/h). The ultimate version, however, was the Ruddspeed 2.6-litre Ford-powered edition, available from 1961, which could be tuned up to 170 bhp. Even so, just 732 of these gorgeous machines were made up to 1962, when the Cobra took precedence at AC (see page 198).

One of the most graceful cars of an era not altogether lacking in beautiful sporting machinery, the Ace married Italianate styling with a robust chassis designed by racing-car engineer John Tojeiro. The Ace tag is due to be revived with a new AC sports car based on the Mercedes-Benz-backed Smart Roadster.

1953 ARMSTRONG-SIDDELEY SAPPHIRE/STAR SAPPHIRE

When they introduced the new Sapphire 346 at the 1952 London Motor Show, Armstrong-Siddeley's directors were worried. Its W.O. Bentley-conceived 3.4-litre, twin-cam straight-six engine produced an easy 120 (later 150) bhp, which, they feared, was at odds with the stately styling. As *Motor* explained a year on, when the car had entered production: 'It was thought that too much emphasis on performance might have an adverse effect on the class of owner to which this make has hitherto appealed, and the potentialities of the new power unit were therefore deliberately not exploited to the full.' That this most traditional of British motor manufacturers should bring out a large saloon that could top 95 mph (153 km/h) and cover a quarter of a mile (400 m) from a standing start in 20 seconds raised more than a few eyebrows.

Apart from the decent turn of speed, the Sapphire was anything but showy. The front doors were hinged at the rear in true pre-war style, while below the imposing façade sat a sturdy ladderframe chassis. Inside it was all wood and leather but without any ostentation beyond the display of mere wealth. An even larger version, the Star Sapphire, arrived in 1955, its engine bored out to 3990 cc in 1959. A total of 7246 Sapphires and 1284 Star Sapphires were made. But plans for a new 5-litre V8 engine were killed off, while the MkII edition of the Star Sapphire, due to take its bow at the 1960 London Motor Show, remained unique. In 1959 Armstrong-Siddeley Motors had merged with Bristol Aero Engines to become Bristol-Siddeley Engines, and after a disastrous foray into the more mainstream saloon-car arena, automobile production ended for good in September 1960 as directors chose to concentrate on the aero industry, which was more lucrative. The company was taken over by Rolls-Royce in 1967.

Impeccably made and powerful thanks to the engine designed by W.O. Bentley, the Star Sapphire would prove to be Armstrong-Siddeley's last automobile as the company's attention focused on the aviation industry.

1953 ASTON MARTIN DB3S

The record speaks for itself: over the course of four years Aston Martin's sublime DB3S started thirty-five major races and scored fifteen outright wins, thirteen seconds and seven third places. That it was also among the prettiest sports cars of the 1950s is in itself a significant achievement, considering the challengers.

After finding success with the DB2 (see p. 117), Aston Martin followed through with the slab-sided DB3. While purpose-built for competition, it was never a serious threat to the Jaguar C-type, largely because of its weight. A new car was needed for the 1953 season: enter the DB3S. With a substantially revised chassis, stumpier wheelbase and narrowed tracks front and rear, the new iteration was significantly lighter – 1850 lb (839 kg) against 2010 lb (912 kg) for the outgoing car – while an increase in displacement to 2.9 litres meant a handy 182 bhp (later up to 237 bhp) from the existing straight-six engine.

Particularly noticeable was the use of a gothic arch in shaping the front and rear wings, a feature that not only sharpened up the car's appearance but also added strength. Nor were the cutaway front wings mere styling gimmicks: a heat shield was installed between the radiator and the engine to deflect hot air from the coolant and dissipate it behind the front wheels.

This particular example, DB3S/9, was one of the last of the line editions. Stirling Moss and Peter Collins drove it to second place in the 1956 Le Mans 24 Hour Race and later that year Moss went one better in the Daily Herald Trophy at Oulton Park, Cheshire. For the following season, the car was raced only sporadically as the DBR1 took precedence in the factory team. By 1958 it had been sold to Ampol Oil of Australia and was campaigned with great success – eight wins from nine starts – by David McKay.

With the DB3S, Aston Martin took the fight to Continental rivals Ferrari and Maserati and routinely beat them in sprint races. That it was exceptionally pretty, as well as fast, was a happy by-product.

Left: Nominally a road car, the DB3S had a two-seater cabin with a modicum of instrumentation and not much else. Head fairing was in place to offset buffeting at speed.

Opposite: The car's glorious outline was the work of underrated stylist Frank Feeley, and employed as much rational thinking as artistic abstraction.

This example of the DB3S was driven to second place at Le Mans in 1956 and enjoyed further competition success in Australia when driven by David McKay.

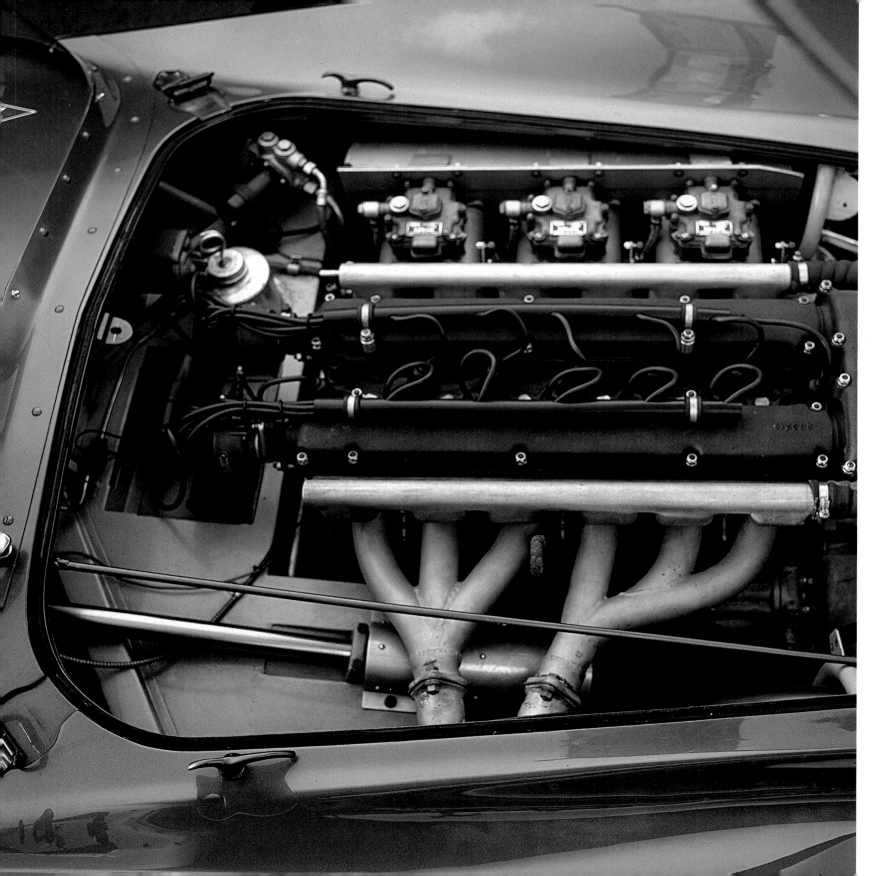

The car's 2.9-litre straight-six engine produced up to 237 bhp, although this was some way less than many overseas rivals.

1953 MG TF MIDGET

Ironically, for a model that is now so coveted among marque devotees and a source of inspiration for replica manufacturers the world over, the TF was a flop first time around. Even within parent company BMC (British Motor Corporation), it was deemed by many as little more than a cynical way of flogging a dead horse one last time. It was a sad end to the illustrious T-series, an avenue in marque lore that a certain amount of revisionism has glossed over: it wasn't that the TF was a bad car, just that it was an anachronism that time and fashion had left behind.

After the TD had proved such a success, especially Stateside where it had been an outstanding performer, a certain level of managerial indifference hobbled MG, preventing it from consolidating its lead in the market. Instead of taking the fight to new challengers from Triumph and Austin-Healey, it chose to repeat the same basic formula: to rework a car to a design that was pre-war in outlook, rather than manufacture the prototype of what ultimately became the MGA (see page 153), and which was already in the stocks. The TF – there never was a TE – was essentially a TD with the same type of chassis, suspension, brakes, engine and transmission. Outwardly it was still ye olde MG, the most obvious changes being to the front end, where the radiator grille was lowered and raked back for a lower bonnet-line. The headlights were faired in rather than separately mounted, and a new valance filled the gap between the base of the rear-sited fuel tanks and the bumper.

But MG was fooling no one, as the sales figures bore out. To 1955, just 6200 of the entry-level 1250-cc car were sold, with the last-gasp 1466-cc, 85-mph (137-km/h) TF1500 model accounting for a further 3400. These days, thirty years' worth of replicas from the likes of RMB, Hudson, Naylor and Alternative Cars probably account for just as many.

Pre-war in outlook and design, the TF wasn't a roaring success in its time. It's ironic, then, that it's now hugely sought-after and that countless replicas are available.

1954 AUSTIN-HEALEY 100S

Unquestionably the most desirable of all Austin-Healeys, the 100S was the culmination of lessons learned developing earlier variations on the theme in competition. To use a contemporary euphemism, these were 'special test cars', so called to avoid displaying any overt interest in motor sport, since parent company BMC had no official racing programme.

Launched at the 1954 London Motor Show, the 100S (the S designation inspired by a successful outing in the Sebring 12 Hour Race that year) outwardly appeared much like the regular Austin-Healey 100 save for a different grille and creases that emanated from the front wheel arches and continued the length of the flanks. It was, however, a significantly more specialized machine. Whereas ordinary 100s were assembled at BMC's Longbridge factory at a rate of around a hundred a week, this road-going racer was largely hand-built at the Donald Healey Motor Company's Warwick premises and bodied in aluminium (in place of the usual steel). The chassis was reinforced with extra gusseting to stop flexing, Dunlop disc brakes were added and a special Weslake cylinder head now sat atop the 2.6-litre, four-cylinder engine. Factory figures quoted a top speed of 118 mph (190 km/h) and a 0–60 mph (100 km/h) time of 7.8 seconds.

The 100S was a true giant-slayer. Stirling Moss and Lance Macklin gave the model its competition baptism in the 1955 Sebring 12 Hours, and finished sixth overall behind a Jaguar D-type, two Ferraris and a brace of Maseratis. This was a tremendous performance against cars with twice the horsepower. A couple of months later George Abecassis won his class in the Mille Miglia aboard his privateer entry. At the end of the year, the 100S was dropped from the line-up after just fifty-five cars had been made, only six of which were sold on the home market.

Although outwardly similar to its mass-production siblings, the 100S was very much a racing car. At the rear, the quick-release filler cap offers all the racer reference points. From front on, the smaller grille is the most obvious deviation from the regular 100 model.

The lack of bumpers lends a purposeful air to the 100S. Distinct from other 100s, the 100S was built by hand and bodied in aluminium rather than steel.

Not lavishly equipped, and with tiny 'fly screens' in place of a regular windshield, the 100S is every inch the road-going racer. The cockpit is comfortable enough, despite being denuded of all weight-adding additions.

1954　JAGUAR D-TYPE

An aesthetic tour de force with an outstanding technical pedigree, the D-type remains one of *the* great motor-sport icons. On smooth, fast-flowing circuits it bested all-comers and made the Le Mans 24 Hour Race its own, with victories from 1955 to 1957, and 1954 and 1958 only near-misses. This being a Jaguar, it was also an off-the-peg racer, with fifty-three being sold to privateers.

The car's structure was state of the art at the time: a stress-bearing monocoque consisting of two bulkheads joined by longitudinal tunnels, the whole wrapped in a riveted aluminium skin to create a structure akin to an aircraft's fuselage. A front subframe of square-section tubing carried the proven 3.4-litre (later 3.8-litre) twin-cam straight-six engine, four-speed gearbox and torsion bar suspension. At the rear, a rather more prosaic frame carried the live rear axle, transverse torsion bar springing and trailing arms. Of particular note was the use of Dunlop disc brakes on all four wheels, driven by a servo-like device at the back of the gearbox. This was at a time when most rivals used drum brakes. The outline was penned by aerodynamicist Malcolm Sayer, and particular care was taken to reduce drag underneath the car. For the 1955 season, factory racers were fitted with a longer, more pointed nose, which increased top speed further to around 180 mph (290 km/h), and a large vertical fin was fitted to the head fairing to aid stability.

At the end of 1955 Jaguar officially pulled out of motor racing, with the factory-blessed Ecurie Ecosse team picking up the mantle as Le Mans challengers. Following its withdrawal, a number of partially completed D-types remained unsold and, in an attempt to recoup some of his investment, Jaguar principal Sir William Lyons decided to convert a number to full road-going configuration. In total, just sixteen of these XK-SS variants were made before a fire at the Browns Lane factory in Coventry destroyed the remaining chassis.

Continuing where the C-type left off, Jaguar's D-type was hugely successful in long-distance races. Nominally a road car, it has a surprisingly comfortable driving position, but for passengers it's agony.

1955 MGA

Following the arrival of the modish Triumph TR2 and Austin-Healey 100 in 1953, MG's insistence on building different variations of essentially the same car for aeons suddenly seemed decidedly old-fashioned. The TF was patently pre-war in spirit, and if the marque was to regain lost ground, especially in the United States, where its reputation was flagging, it needed more than a reworked 1930s design. The MGA, introduced at the 1955 Frankfurt Motor Show, was anything but antiquated. Its beautiful, deliciously rounded body was perfectly proportioned and of the moment, while its 1489-cc four-cylinder B-series engine – borrowed from the recently announced MG Magnette saloon – produced bags of torque and a healthy 68 bhp (soon upped to 72). Suspension was independent, with coil springs and wishbones at the front and a rigid axle with semi-elliptic springs at the rear. Steering was by rack and pinion.

The car's styling borrowed heavily from a rebodied MG TD designed by Syd Evener and entered by George Phillips in the 1951 Le Mans 24 Hour Race. Before the A's official launch, a trio of experimental aluminium-bodied prototypes were entered in the 1955 running, finishing in twelfth and seventeenth overall, the third car crashing and ending the racing career of its driver, Dick Jacobs.

The A was an immediate success, with a coupé edition being added to the range in 1956 and a high-performance twin-cam model joining the line-up two years later. The twin-cam version featured an aluminium high-compression double overhead-cam cylinder head on the B-series engine and produced 108 bhp. Unfortunately, it soon gained notoriety for fragility and was dropped in 1960. By this time, the standard car had received a useful performance hike, capacity being upped to 1558 cc. In 1961 displacement was increased again to 1622 cc, before production ended a year later as the MGA made way for the MGB. By this time 101,801 had been made of all types.

This example physically replicates an MGA that competed at Le Mans in 1955. The original was involved in a horrifying crash that almost claimed the life of its driver, Dick Jacobs.

1957 LISTER-JAGUAR

By his own admission, Brian Lister was never a great racing driver. He did, however, build some fabulous racing cars. After a successful stint as a drummer in a jazz band, The Downbeats, he joined the family engineering firm in the early 1950s and began dabbling in motor sport with a Morgan 4/4. This in turn led to him mating a Tojeiro chassis with a JAP V-twin motorcycle engine, the resultant Asteroid (although some suggested 'Haemorrhoid') doing its best to kill him on several occasions.

At the end of 1953 Lister began laying the foundations for his eponymous marque after persuading his father to fork out £1500 and allow him six months' leave so that he could prove himself as a car manufacturer. The resultant publicity from any competition success would be beneficial to George Lister & Sons, he promised.

Thanks to tuning whizz Don Moore and devastatingly quick driver Archie Scott Brown, the marque soon entered into legend. After building cars powered by MG, Bristol and Maserati engines, Lister-Jaguar produced its first vehicle after British Petroleum (in a bid to better the Esso-backed Aston Martin factory team) made an approach to sponsor a sports-car competition programme.

With a tubular-steel spaceframe chassis and 3.4-litre straight-six engine, the 'works' car won twelve races from fourteen starts during 1957. Such success led to around a dozen chassis being sold for the following season (some with Chevrolet V8 power), although Brian Lister began to lose interest following the tragic death of his close friend Scott Brown at Spa. For 1959 a new body was created by Frank Costin, but the writing was on the wall. The marque was quietly dropped in 1960. The particular example shown on these pages was sold new to Kjell Qvale of San Francisco and raced by Jack Flaherty. It is currently owned by a Swiss collector.

The scourge of better-financed factory teams from the likes of Aston Martin and Jaguar, Listers ruled sprint-format sports-car races in Britain during the mid- to late 1950s.

155

Below: Its famously curvy outline earned the Lister-Jaguar the nickname 'Knobbly'. Aluminium bodywork is mounted on a chassis comprising two large-diameter tubes, with tubular formers to support the panel-work.

Opposite: This particular Lister was sold new to San Francisco motor mogul Kjell Qvale, and was raced on the East Coast of the United States in the late 1950s and early 1960s. It is currently owned by a Swiss collector.

1957 LOTUS ELITE

Like that other great colossus of motor sport, Enzo Ferrari, Colin Chapman was never really interested in road cars. They were a means to an end, a method of perpetuating the Lotus marque and raising enough revenue with which to go racing. The Elite represented Chapman's desire to be seen as a major player: he craved a GT with a race-proven engine and suspension set-up, all within an aerodynamically efficient silhouette. This he achieved and more.

When introduced at the 1957 Earls Court Motor Show, the Elite caught everyone off guard. Lotus was barely ten years old, yet this achingly pretty sports car was a technical tour de force. The concept of an all-glassfibre monocoque was entirely new, the wind-cheating shape proffering a drag coefficient of just 0.29 cd. Astonishingly, the outline was the work of an accountant, Peter Kirwan-Taylor, his remarkable offering being tweaked and honed by aerodynamicist Frank Costin.

Powered by an all-alloy Coventry Climax FWE engine – originally designed as a fireman's pump that could be carried by two men – the Elite made the most of its meagre 1216-cc displacement. It initially produced just 75 bhp (up to 105 bhp in time), but the car's featherweight construction – only 1484 lb (673 kg) – and rev-happy engine ensured that it could exceed 110 mph (177 km/h). And despite being conceived as a road car, the Elite naturally attracted the attention of the competition fraternity. It won first time out at Silverstone in May 1958 in the hands of Ian Walker, and found greater fame in the Le Mans 24 Hour Race when in 1959 the Peter Lumsden/Peter Riley entry finished an amazing eighth overall and took the 1500-cc category prize. It was the first of six consecutive class triumphs in the endurance classic.

Unfortunately, the labour-intensive method of construction ensured that money was lost on every one of the 1050 Elites made up until 1963.

The world's first glassfibre monocoque, the Elite represented Lotus's first faltering steps into the production-car market. It was too costly to build ever to return a profit.

Below: It sounds unlikely, but the Elite's delicate outline was the work of an accountant, Peter Kirwan-Taylor. He was also responsible for the short-lived Citroën Bijou.

Opposite: A small frontal area and close attention to airflow resulted in a remarkably aerodynamic profile. This ensured that, despite the small engine capacity, the Elite was indecently quick.

Despite being conceived as a road car, the Elite proved to be a formidable racing car, with class wins at Le Mans. Elite drivers included such stars as Jim Clark, Les Leston and Lotus founder, Colin Chapman.

1959 ASTON MARTIN DB4GT

Unveiled at the 1958 Paris Salon, the Aston Martin DB4 represented a major leap forward over outgoing models, thanks to its new pressed-steel chassis, 3.7-litre twin-cam straight-six engine and all-round disc brakes. It was also extremely beautiful; the customarily brilliant Touring of Milan had turned out a perfectly balanced outline that was offered in both open and closed forms. To the unversed, the GT variant appeared outwardly similar save for the Perspex-shrouded headlights, which would remain a DB constant until 1970. It was, however, a high-caffeine iteration, one that made its first public appearance at Silverstone on 2 May 1959, when Stirling Moss won the BRDC GT race in the DP199/1 prototype.

In fact, the GT, launched officially at the 1959 London Motor Show, differed substantially from the regular DB4. Having won the World Sportscar Championship, the marque officially pulled out of racing in 1959, and general manager John Wyer conceived the new strain as a means of providing a car for privateers. Chief engineer Harold Beach set to, shortening the wheelbase by 5 in. (127 mm) and manufacturing the bodywork from thinner-gauge aluminium. These alterations and others accounted for a saving of 185 lb (84 kg) over the standard car. Beneath the skin, engine capacity remained at 3670 cc (although some cars were enlarged to 3750 cc), but the new version was given a modified cylinder head and triple twin-choke Weber carburettors. Power output was a healthy 302 bhp at 6000 rpm, a sizeable increase over the probably optimistic 240 bhp of the standard DB4. Factory figures claimed a top speed of 153 mph (246 km/h) and 0–60 mph (100 km/h) in 6.1 seconds; acceleration to 100 mph (160 km/h) from standstill; and braking to a complete stop in under 20 seconds.

Although Moss was never able to vanquish Ferrari's 250-series cars in long-distance events, he came out on top at Nassau in 1959, and DB4GTs also won races, sprints and hillclimbs as far afield as Brands Hatch and Bonneville.

Although routinely held up as a paragon of British design 'cool', the DB4GT's outline was actually the work of the chief stylist at Touring of Milan, Federico Formenti.

From the fluting around the rear glazing to the surprisingly long overhang, the DB4GT was a work of beauty. Many of its styling cues were carried over on to its successor, the DB5.

According to the factory, the strident 3670-cc straight-six engine produced over 300 bhp (which was probably an exaggeration). Even so, it was powerful enough to ensure race wins.

1959 AUSTIN SE7EN MINI/MORRIS MINI COOPER

The Mini never made any money over four decades of production. That's the problem with blazing trails: it's always those tagging along after the bugs have been ironed out who profit. And the Mini and its Cooper derivative were revolutionary. Conceived by visionary engineer Alec Issigonis, this design icon represented BMC's response to the Suez Crisis of 1956, when fuel economy became all-important (see Introduction, p. 20).

'Project ADO15' (Austin Design Office) housed the entirely conventional four-cylinder A-series engine, but departed from the norm by having it mounted sideways, with front-wheel drive and the engine-oil-lubricated, four-speed transmission mounted in the sump. The transverse engine location, which has since become the standard configuration for virtually every small car, saved precious cabin space: the entire car measured only 10 ft (3 m) long, around 80 per cent of which was given over to the passenger compartment. The suspension set-up, devised by Alex Moulton, used rubber cones instead of conventional springs, which lent it almost go-kart levels of handling.

Arguably the world's first truly classless car, and the epitome of 1960s cool, the Mini took an entirely new direction after Formula One team boss John Cooper turned his attention to tuning the little car. Mini Coopers slayed their larger rivals in competition, the S edition scoring outright wins at the Monte Carlo Rally in 1964, 1965 and 1967. It actually came first in 1966 but was disqualified for a spurious headlight infringement (as was the fourth-placed Lotus-Cortina). The award went to the fifth-placed Citroën DS, which had equally 'illegal' illumination (but then it was a French car).

The Cooper tag was dropped in 1971, but it had such resonance with the motoring public that the moniker was briefly revived in 1990 under the RSP (Rover Special Projects) banner. It proved so popular that a new Mini Cooper went into full-scale production in 1991.

In a masterpiece of packaging, the Mini's four-cylinder A-series engine was mounted transversely to free up cabin space.

Opposite: Never has a car's name been more appropriate: the Mini was just that. It was a perfect town car and, in tuned Cooper form as here, a formidable race and rally weapon.

Below: Exposed door hinges and sliding side glazing lent a slightly utilitarian air to the Mini, although 'Minilite' wheels, as here, brought a racy edge to the Cooper edition.

Below: The Mini was perhaps the first classless car, beloved by pensioners as well as rock stars. Along with the Jaguar E-type, it was a 1960s automotive icon, but it lost its maker a fortune.

Opposite: The Mini's designer, Alec Issigonis, insisted on a basic cabin. He especially hated car radios, claiming that they were an unnecessary – and dangerous – distraction for drivers.

1959 JAGUAR MKII

Jaguar's original sports saloon has undergone a critical re-evaluation of late. It is now most widely recognized for its appearance in the hugely popular TV series *Inspector Morse*. An odd choice of car for a cerebral, white-haired detective, perhaps, since in its heyday the MkII was less a dignified conveyance for intellectuals and more a favourite of armed robbers. The top-of-the-range 3.8-litre edition was the perfect getaway car. The British police force figured that it too needed the MkII in its armoury, and it wasn't long before it was similarly equipped. This was probably not the sort of image that Jaguar founder Sir William Lyons had sought, but the gangster association undoubtedly lent the MkII a certain shady cachet.

The MkII's roots can be traced to the 2.4 saloon (retrospectively known as the MkI), which went on sale in 1956. Projected to fill the gap between the XK sports cars and the gargantuan MkVII, it was notable for breaking with Jaguar tradition in being of monocoque construction. Powered by the legendary XK straight-six engine (originally in 2483-cc form), the model took off apace with the introduction of a 3.4-litre variant a year later.

The MkII, when it appeared in October 1959, was outwardly similar but had been extensively re-engineered. Major improvements included a wider rear track and Dunlop disc brakes as standard. The MkII retained the 2.4- and 3.4-litre engine options, but it was the arrival of the 3781-cc edition that really paved the way for legendary status. In 1960 *The Autocar* recorded an almost unbelievable 126 mph (202 km/h) and 0–60 mph (100 km/h) in 8.5 seconds, which made it the fastest saloon car in the world, and a bargain at just £1800. It defined an entire genre of automobile, paving the way for the even more remarkable XJ6 in 1968.

Beloved by armed robbers and racing drivers alike, the MkII was a true sporting saloon that, in classic Jaguar style, offered unrivalled pace for the money.

1961 ASTON MARTIN DB4GT ZAGATO

Despite Zagato being more than capable of the odd credibility chasm, its take on the DB4GT remains one of *the* landmark car designs. Styled by the youthful, self-taught Ercole Spada (later head of design at BMW), the car was unveiled at the 1960 London Motor Show. Plans called for a limited run of twenty-five cars to be constructed; in fact, just twenty were made (two of them sharing the same chassis number) from 1961 to 1963. No two were alike, vagaries of the coachbuilt method of manufacture and individual whims of customers accounting for differences from car to car.

The Zagato was built to challenge the Ferrari 250GT SWB on the race track. Rolling chassis were dispatched to the Zagato factory in Milan to be clothed with lightweight aluminium bodies. The car retained the DB4GT's straight-six engine, but power was increased to 314 bhp, so acceleration was vivid, the 0–60 mph (100 km/h) dash taking just 6.1 seconds, and it could reach up to 153 mph (246 km/h) overall. Ultimately, however, the Zagato failed to shine at international level. The first example was entered in the 1962 Le Mans 24 Hour Race in the hands of Mike Salmon and Ian Baillie, but it retired in the ninth hour with a holed piston. The two most famous Zagato drivers were future double Formula One champion Jim Clark and Aston stalwart Roy Salvadori, both of whom drove for John Ogier's Essex Racing Stable, with wins at national level.

At the height of the late 1980s classic-car investment boom, one DB4GT Zagato sold for a record £1.7 million. In 1987 the co-owners of Aston Martin, Peter Livanos and Victor Gauntlett, decided to build four more, using up chassis numbers left unallocated from the earlier batch. They were constructed in the workshops of ex-Zagato employee Mario Galbiatti and were known as Sanction 2 cars.

The muscular Zagato take on the DB4GT is now routinely cited as a styling masterclass, but it was slow to catch on at the time. Lightweight aluminium panel-work meant a 40-lb (18-kg) saving over the regular offering from Touring of Milan.

No two Zagato DB4GTs were ever exactly alike, owing largely to the handmade nature of their construction and whims of individual customers. Styling was the work of Ercole Spada.

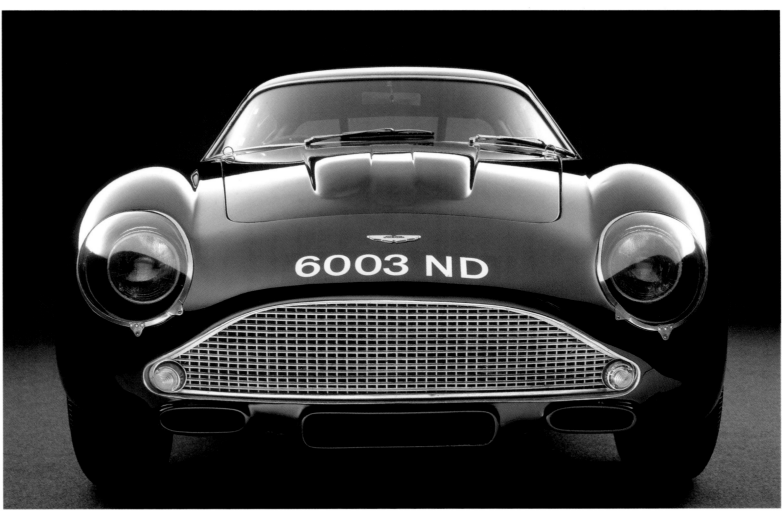

Left: Like the particular model shown here, most Zagato DB4GTs were destined for competition use. The low roofline encroached on cabin space, but the basic architecture is carried over from the regular production DB4.

Opposite: This example was campaigned in the Le Mans 24 Hour Race in 1962 and 1963 by Jean Kerguen and Jacques Dewes (using the pseudonym 'Franc'). Sadly, it failed to complete the distance on both occasions.

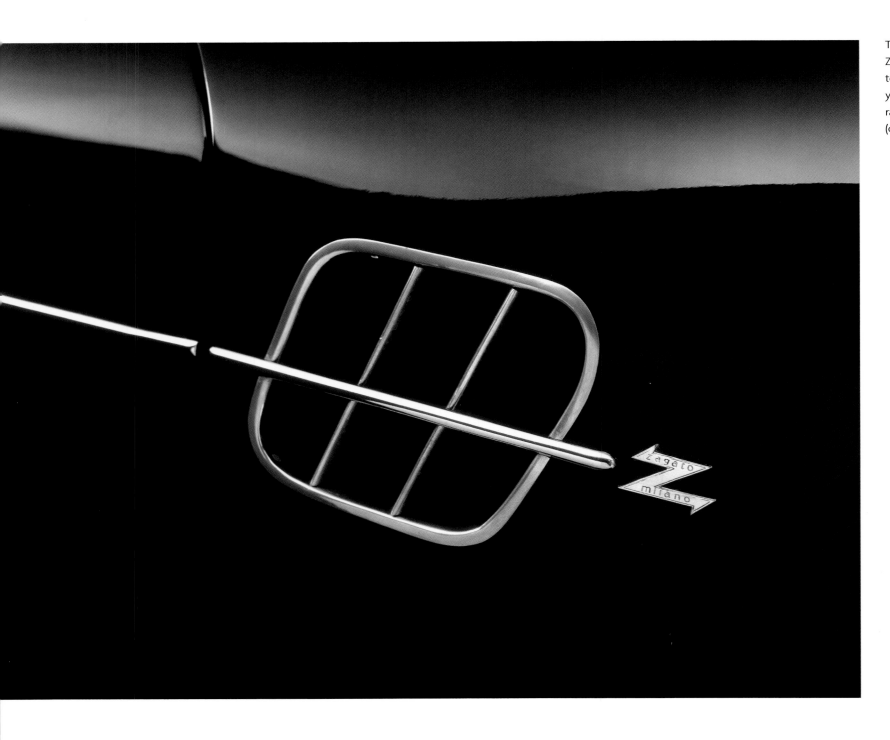

This side air vent is larger than on most Zagato Astons and was altered in 1964 to dissipate under-bonnet heat. That year the car won the Route du Nord rally in France. The straight-six engine (opposite) nominally produces 314 bhp.

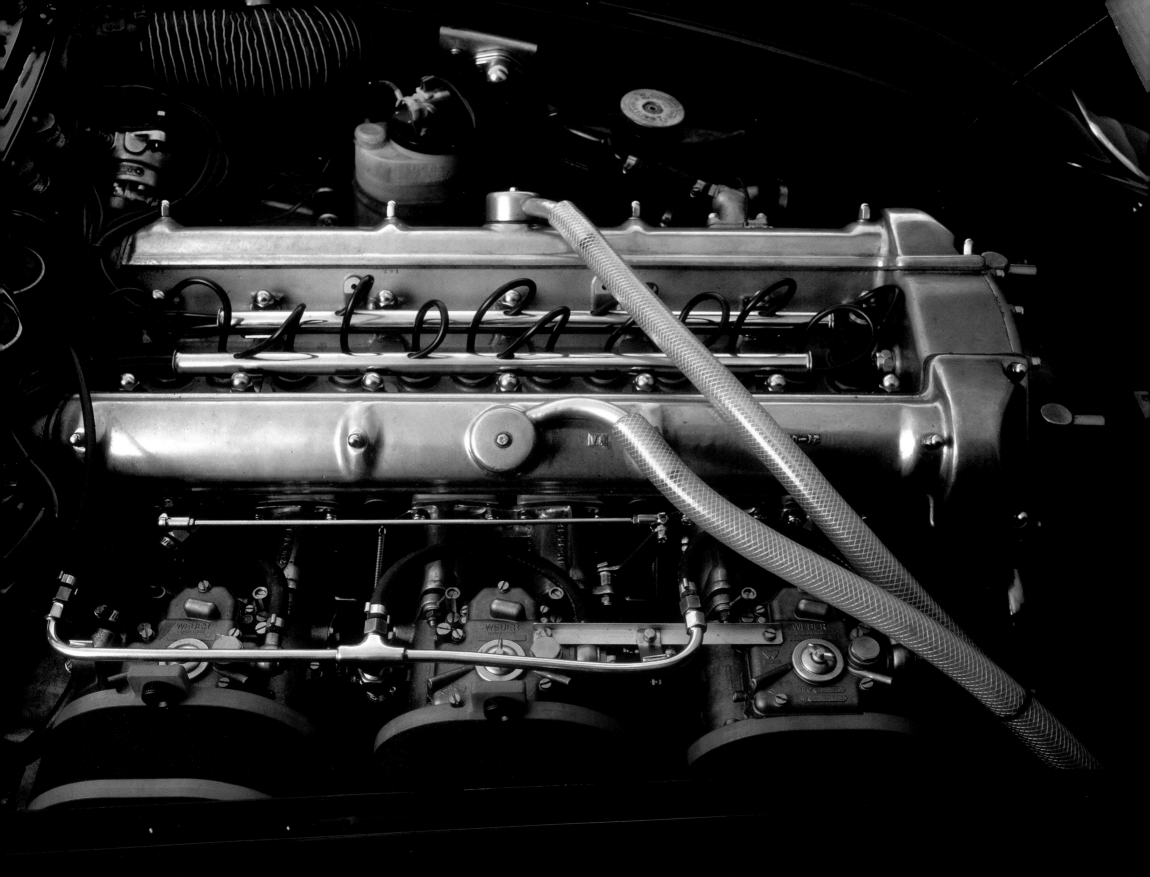

1961 JAGUAR E-TYPE

As compliments go, it's a big one. Legend has it that Ferrari rushed its 250GTO into being out of fear that the E-type would clean up in sports-car racing. While the Maranello car was a pure-bred competition tool, however, the Coventry machine was intended for road use. That it handily doubled as a racing car was an added bonus.

Few cars made such an instant impression as the E-type (XK-E in the United States). Reporters from *The Autocar* famously drove the factory demonstrator to the 1961 Geneva Salon, at which it made its debut, and recorded a top speed of 150 mph (241 km/h). While there is little doubt that this particular example had been slightly tweaked – certainly no production car ever quite matched this figure – it was clear that the E-type represented a quantum leap forward in performance. Not only that, it also maintained Jaguar's legacy of value for money. Here was a car that was comfortably faster than most exotica, with advanced monocoque construction and independent rear suspension, yet it easily undercut them all. Back in 1961, a coupé could have been yours for £1550, if you didn't mind waiting. Ferrari's 250GT was £6600; the Aston Martin DB4, £4000. Little wonder that demand for the E-type outstripped supply.

Routinely lauded as one of *the* landmark car designs, the original E-type continued where the XK-series had left off with dizzying beauty, a plush – if difficult to get into – cabin and an electrifying pace.

The E-type was offered in coupé or roadster configurations; its delectable styling was largely the work of aerodynamicist Malcolm Sayer, and was inspired by Touring's Disco Volante ('flying saucer') designs for Alfa Romeo. It was launched with a 3.8-litre version of the classic XK twin-cam, straight-six engine. Displacement was enlarged to 4.2 litres three years later, and the last of the line series featured 5.3-litre V12 power.

Despite having no official works involvement in motor sport, Jaguar assisted several privateers, which led to the construction of twelve 'lightweight' editions. Distinct from the road cars, these featured aluminium body/monocoque assemblies. Power came from an all-aluminium straight-six engine with a wide-angle cylinder head and Lucas fuel injection. The most notable result was ninth overall in the 1963 Le Mans 24 Hour Race for the Briggs Cunningham entry.

While some design critics feel that the height of the windscreen interrupts the lines, nobody can fault the E-type's rear view: there isn't a line wrong on it. The tailgate is hinged to open like a door rather than a hatchback. Later iterations would lose the styling purity, with larger light clusters mounted beneath the bumper.

Ovoid grille, recessed headlights and prominent bonnet bulge all conspire to create an aggressive presence. The bonnet flips forward in one piece to reveal the classic 3.8-litre XK straight-six engine. Capacity was soon increased to 4.2 litres, and later iterations featured 5.3-litre V12 power.

Jaguar boss Sir William Lyons styled cars more by eye and gut feeling than with a pencil, relying on design ally Malcolm Sayer to ensure that the car was aerodynamically efficient. Although exceptionally pretty, the E-type never did cut through the air cleanly, the nose lifting at high speeds.

The debate has raged for years: which is more beautiful, the E-type roadster or the coupé? As is demonstrated by the roadster shown here and the coupé on previous pages, both were more than a match for the best Italian exotica of the day. For beauty and outright performance, the E-type seriously outdid not only Italian styling but also elite British rival Aston Martin.

1961 TRIUMPH TR4

Following an abortive attempt at taking over Morgan, the Standard-Triumph Motor Company made a bid for sporting glory with the TR2. Introduced in 1953, this snub-nosed roadster sold reasonably well before it was replaced with the similar TR3 range. Having made inroads into MG's heartland territory, Triumph introduced the more grown-up TR4 in 1961. It was essentially a rebodied TR3A with styling by prolific Italian designer Giovanni Michelotti, but its attractive outline did away with the traditional cutaway doors and side-curtains; in their place came an of-the-minute silhouette with a higher waistline and wind-up windows.

Despite a wider track front and rear, and larger bodywork that accounted for an extra 12 in. (30 cm) in length over its predecessor, the TR4 retained the same basic foundations of earlier Triumphs. Particularly novel, though, was the optional 'Surrey' roof, a steel hardtop with a lift-out centre section that pre-dated Porsche's similar Targa design. Power came from a 2-litre (later 2.2-litre) four-cylinder engine, which allowed a top speed of 102 mph (164 km/h) and a 0–60 mph (100 km/h) time of 10.9 seconds. Rugged and reliable, the TR4 maintained Triumph's participation in rallying, although its heft ultimately got in the way of outright success.

In 1965 the TR4A arrived. Although outwardly little different, the new model featured independent rear suspension (just to confuse historians, however, some cars were sold, mostly in the United States, with the old live axle arrangement). Unfortunately, while this arrangement added refinement, it also added weight and blunted performance. By 1968, 25,465 had been made, along with 40,304 TR4s (which ceased production in 1964). The rarest derivative was the Dove GTR4, a coachbuilt coupé crafted for Standard-Triumph distributor L.F. Dove of Wimbledon by Thomas Harrington of Hove, Sussex. Only fifty or so were made.

Styled by Italian Giovanni Michelotti, the TR4 was an altogether prettier car than the preceding TR3, although it shared the same rugged chassis and basic running gear.

Handsome in profile, and fun to drive, the TR4 nonetheless had its faults, not least the cramped cabin. Even so, it was popular at home and in overseas markets, and also maintained Triumph's involvement in rallying.

1962   AC COBRA

Oh, the irony. During its production life the Cobra was a commercial failure. Just 996 of all types were made and, by the end, dealers could barely give them away. Fast-forward to the present, and the Cobra is the most replicated car on the planet. Time was when a Cobra owner would cringe and recoil when an enquiry was made as to its validity. Nowadays onlookers simply presume anything wearing a Cobra badge is a fake. 'Cobra' has become a generic term, a badge of convenience for kit-car manufacturers. More copies are now made in twelve months than Carroll Shelby, the car's Texan instigator, managed to produce of the original in seven years.

After a successful racing career that included victory in the Le Mans 24 Hour Race, Shelby toured various car manufacturers, touting his vision of a sports car. Rather than creating one from scratch, he reasoned that the insertion of a large-capacity American V8 engine into a lightweight European chassis would make for a compelling sports car. Austin-Healey was his first choice, but his advances were rebuffed, while Chevrolet was less than enthusiastic about handing over its engines, fearing competition for its Corvette model. Fortunately for Shelby, Ford was more forthcoming and agreed to furnish its latest 4.2-litre (later 4.7-litre) unit, while AC found a new lease of life for its Ace. The marriage of the two seemingly disparate constituents resulted in the Cobra.

From 1962 to 1967 Shelby America received AC chassis from Thames Ditton, Surrey, and inserted engines and running gear at its California facility. The car's success in motor sport heightened its profile, and the Rip Chords' song 'Hey, Little Cobra' brought it immortality. But it still didn't sell in large numbers, despite the arrival of the 7-litre 427 model in 1965. AC continued building its own variant until 1969, when the Cobra was quietly killed off. By the end of the following decade, the market for replicas had begun to flourish.

Truly deserving of the tag 'legendary', the Cobra – here in Fédération Internationale de l'Automobile race trim – was an Anglo-American hybrid that was as fast as it was loud. If any inanimate object could be said to exude charisma, it would be this one.

Riding on cast-magnesium Halibrand wheels, arches flared to accommodate them, the Cobra is brutally attractive. The narrow cockpit ensures that the driver is effectively sitting on a chassis rail, which makes for a bumpy ride.

The cockpit is geared to competition, despite having an attractive alloy-spoked steering wheel, which is more usually seen in road cars.

Devised by a Texan and built by a firm in Surrey, the Cobra gave a new lease of life to the AC Ace, on which it is based. The insertion of a small-block Ford V8 engine and a change of name created a Ferrari-baiting marvel that still captivates.

Left: Cobras always were basic: exposed aluminium covers the transmission tunnel, and there are few luxury fripperies in the stripped-out racer cockpit.

Opposite: A 4.7-litre Ford V8 running on Weber carburettors powers this Cobra. The ultimate edition – the monstrous 427 – featured 7-litre power, but it handled like a wayward shopping trolley.

1963 ASTON MARTIN DB5

Unarguably it remains the greatest act of product placement in movie history. The image of the Silver Birch Aston Martin was seared into the collective consciousness by being immortalized on celluloid with the coolest spy of them all: James Bond in *Goldfinger*. (In Ian Fleming's novel the hero drove a DB3.) Surprisingly, Aston Martin was the second choice: Jaguar had baulked at the idea of loaning cars to the film's producers, much as it did when the makers of *The Saint* TV series came knocking. In both instances Jaguar lost levels of free global advertising of which manufacturers can usually only dream.

The DB5 maintains its cult following, and is frequently regarded as the quintessential 1960s performance car, but in fact there's nothing especially remarkable about its make-up. Introduced in 1963, the DB5 was essentially a development of the outgoing DB4 Series 5 Vantage, and it looked almost identical. It maintained the exquisite outline and Touring's *superleggera* method of construction. Bigger changes were beneath the skin, principal among them being the adoption of a 4-litre version of the existing straight-six engine (282 bhp) and the option of a five-speed ZF gearbox (which became standard equipment in place of the old four-speed item after the first fifty cars had been built). In regular trim the DB5 could reach 144 mph (231 km/h); sixty-five of the 898 coupés made by 1965 featured the optional Vantage package (triple Weber carburettors and 314 bhp), which meant 150 mph (240 km/h). Just 123 convertible models were made, nineteen of them left-hand drive. The rarest of the breed were the estate cars – or 'shooting brakes' – built by coachbuilder Harold Radford. The first of the twelve made went to Aston Martin's owner, Sir David Brown.

Inextricably linked with James Bond following its appearance in *Goldfinger* in 1964, the DB5 was the perfect automotive accompaniment to the suave super-spy's arsenal.

1963 ELVA MK7/MK7S

During the late 1950s and early 1960s, only Elva matched Lotus as a volume manufacturer of racing cars. By the dawn of the 1970s, following a boom-and-bust existence, the marque had died a quiet death. Today the name (a contraction of the French *elle va*, 'she goes') is all but forgotten, which is a tragedy since such models as the Mk7 proved hugely successful in their time on racing tracks across Europe and North America.

Technically, this diminutive sports racer was fairly typical of the breed, with a light but strong spaceframe chassis that weighed just 73 lb (33 kg), all-round wishbone suspension and a mid-mounted engine – usually of BMW origin – driving the rear wheels via a Hewland gearbox. Wrapped tightly around all this was a very pretty glassfibre body.

Following the model's introduction at the 1963 Racing Car Show in London, Elva instigator Frank Nichols, with the help of US concessionaire Carl Haas and Porsche distributor Ollie Schmidt, pulled off a coup by persuading Porsche to release a supply of its 1.7-litre, four-cam Carrera engines. Porsche had hitherto turned away advances from other suitors, so this move caused much consternation within the German manufacturer's own competition department, which had been unaware of the decision.

The prototype Elva-Porsche made its race debut in September 1963 in the Road America 500 at Elkhart Lake, where Bill Wuesthoff put the car on pole position. He and Augie Pabst went on to score an emphatic win, and Elva immediately received fifteen orders.

In total, twenty-nine Mk7s were made, with Porsche-engined cars being referred to by the Mk7S designation. Despite open hostility by some Porsche insiders, the factory team took delivery of an Elva and equipped it with a Type 771 flat-eight engine for an attempt at the 1964 European Hillclimb Championship. Driver Edgar Barth won the first round at Rossfeld, Germany. In second place, four seconds behind, was a works Porsche 718.

Elva and Porsche were two names inextricably linked with motor sport, yet only Porsche's still resonates. Sadly, Elva's period as a serious player in circuit racing was a brief one.

Opposite: Porsche insiders were reluctant to provide its quad-cam four-cylinder unit to Elva. It represented the first time the German manufacturer had ever directly supplied another marque with its engines.

Below: Pretty Mk7S styling was typical of the better early 1960s production sports-racing cars, with a small frontal area and low cockpit sides. Bodywork was really there only to keep the rain out.

Although few inside Porsche would ever admit it, the Mk7S influenced future generations of the German marque's racing cars. The company went as far as to obtain one that it prepared for the European Hillclimb Championship; it was immediately successful.

1964 MARCOS

God loves a trier, and few tried harder to make a go of building sports cars than Jem Marsh. This former seaman and occasional stunt driver found minor fame during the 1950s 'specials' boom, supplying components and bodyshells to kit-car builders under the Speedex banner. Marcos grew out of collaboration with freelance designer and former Olympic-standard swimmer Frank Costin (Marcos being a contraction of the two men's surnames). Its first car, featuring a timber monocoque and gullwing doors, was known as the Xylon (from the Greek for 'wood'), and was breathtakingly ugly. Early adopters of the model included future triple Formula One world champion Jackie Stewart.

Costin soon departed, and brothers Dennis and Peter Adams refined the car's outline before conceiving a new and altogether less race-orientated strain. Intended as a stopgap while a radical rear-engined car with a central driving position was completed, the new Marcos retained the wooden hull and glassfibre body but deviated from standard Marcos practice in being attractive. The new 1800 caused a furore at the 1964 Racing Car Show in London. The rear-engined project was swiftly dropped, while variations of the production coupé theme continue to this day.

Power came initially from a 1.8-litre Volvo engine, but countless other units found their way under the shapely flip-forward bonnet before the end of the decade, including straight-six Triumph and unlovely Ford V4 engines. When Marcos took on the American market in 1968, the wooden monocoque was abandoned owing to customer resistance, and replaced with a tubular-steel frame.

Throughout this period, money problems meant that the car never realized its potential, although Marsh gamely sought out investors to share his vision. It couldn't last: Marcos folded in 1971, and Marsh operated a business servicing cars for existing owners before reviving the marque ten years later.

Of all the low-volume British sports-car marques, Marcos is the one that has displayed the greatest longevity, give or take the occasional fallow year; this is remarkable, as the car was originally intended only as a stopgap.

Below: The dramatic lines of the Marcos were penned by the remarkable Dennis Adams. The work of this largely unrecognized designer/artist ranges from wrought-iron gates and furniture to pyramid-shaped city cars and ornate off-roaders.

Opposite: The aircraft-inspired dashboard was fitted only to very early cars. Later editions featured a more conventional veneered walnut item; or, as Adams put it, they were 'cheapened with a plank'.

1965 TRIDENT CLIPPER

The Trident marque is inextricably linked with TVR and parent company Grantura Engineering. By the early 1960s TVR's lightweight, if not altogether attractive, sports cars were selling only in small numbers. Company director Bernard Williams reasoned that by producing something prettier, the firm would attract customers. A chance meeting with stylist Trevor Fiore (né Frost) was the start of a tortuous saga.

Fiore produced a design that drew heavily on a stillborn proposal for Lea-Francis dating from 1961. After TVR's directors approved of his ideas, Fiore arranged for Italian coachbuilder Fissore to interpret his brief in time for the 1965 Geneva Salon. The resultant coupé, based on a lengthened TVR Griffith chassis with 4.7-litre Ford V8 power, wowed everyone, the *Daily Telegraph* headlining it as 'the most beautiful car in the world'.

Three more prototypes, including a lone convertible, were built before TVR and Grantura Engineering lurched into bankruptcy. Father and son Arthur and Martin Lilley made a successful rescue bid, in part on the strength of the Trident, only to discover that TVR dealer Bill Last had somehow obtained the rights to that particular car.

Trident the model then became Trident the marque, although understandably without further access to TVR chassis. Last arranged for a supply of Austin-Healey 3000 frames, which were then altered to accommodate the big American engines, and Fiore reworked the styling with Grantura Engineering – now independent of TVR – to produce bodyshells in glassfibre. A Triumph TR6 chassis was substituted once production of the Austin-Healey ended, in 1969.

The Trident Clipper always remained on the fringes of the exotic sports-car market. A sister model, the Venturer, with Ford V6 power, was added to the line-up in 1969, followed by the Triumph-powered Tycoon in 1971, only for Trident Cars to stumble into liquidation in 1972. A recovery attempt in 1976 came to little, and only 130 cars were made before the end of the company, a year later.

The Trident was born of a TVR design study, and its existence was a tortuous one. Cars such as the Clipper (shown here) were built in tiny numbers, often between company crashes – a pity, as the basic product was compelling.

1966   AC 428

It promised much but ultimately failed to deliver. By the mid-1960s, AC was building Cobras for the home market in spits and coughs, but the Anglo-American hybrid was always a Carroll Shelby benefit: AC was little more than a subcontractor, and it was the Texan showman who took the plaudits (see p. 198). The 428 represented a change of direction for the marque: a high-speed luxury grand tourer that belonged to AC alone.

AC company principal Derek Hurlock initially approached the Bertone styling house to design the new car. Unconvinced after initial discussions, he opted instead for Pietro Frua's tiny *carrozzeria*, following an introduction by racing driver Hubert Patthey. A Cobra MkIII chassis was dispatched to Turin to be lengthened and clothed in its new skin. The result bore more than a passing resemblance to Frua's earlier Maserati Mistral project, but the myth that the two cars featured interchangeable body panels was exactly that: a myth. The likeness did, however, raise more than a few eyebrows when the prototype convertible was displayed at the 1965 London Motor Show.

The car looked like a winner, however. A 7-litre V8 engine normally found in a police-spec Ford Galaxie ensured a vivid performance of more than 140 mph (225 km/h), and initial plans called for Frua to build bodies for the first 150 cars until Hurlock arranged for a supplier local to AC's home in Thames Ditton, Surrey. It never happened. By March 1969 only fifty cars had been completed, largely because of industrial unrest in Italy and because variable quality meant that much time was wasted rectifying problems. Factor in the laborious nature of construction, with bare chassis being shipped to Italy for the steel body to be welded on and then returned to Britain for final painting, trimming and insertion of running gear, and delivery dates became a farce. With the fuel crisis of 1973, demand for such thirsty machines dwindled to nothing, and when the 428 was dropped, just eighty had been made, of which fifty-one were coupés.

In styling AC's 7-litre 428, Pietro Frua replicated the lines of his earlier Maserati Mistral design. Beneath the skin, the AC 428 was essentially a lengthened AC Cobra.

Left: The coachbuilt nature of the 428's construction mitigated against volume production. Even so, had it not been for Italian labour disputes and lousy build quality, the 428 might have been made in far greater quantities.

Opposite: The 428's cabin retains an aura of jet-set cool, with gauges clustered behind the classic alloy-spoked steering wheel. The cranked-over gear lever is a reminder of the car's Cobra ancestry.

Left: The 7-litre V8 produced prodigious amounts of power and was normally found in police-spec Ford Galaxies. In the 428 it was a blue-collar retort to highly strung Italian V12s.

Opposite: Arguably the 428's best view is of the rear three-quarters. Unarguably, the fastback styling is elegant. (Note that the pair of AC logos here are not original.)

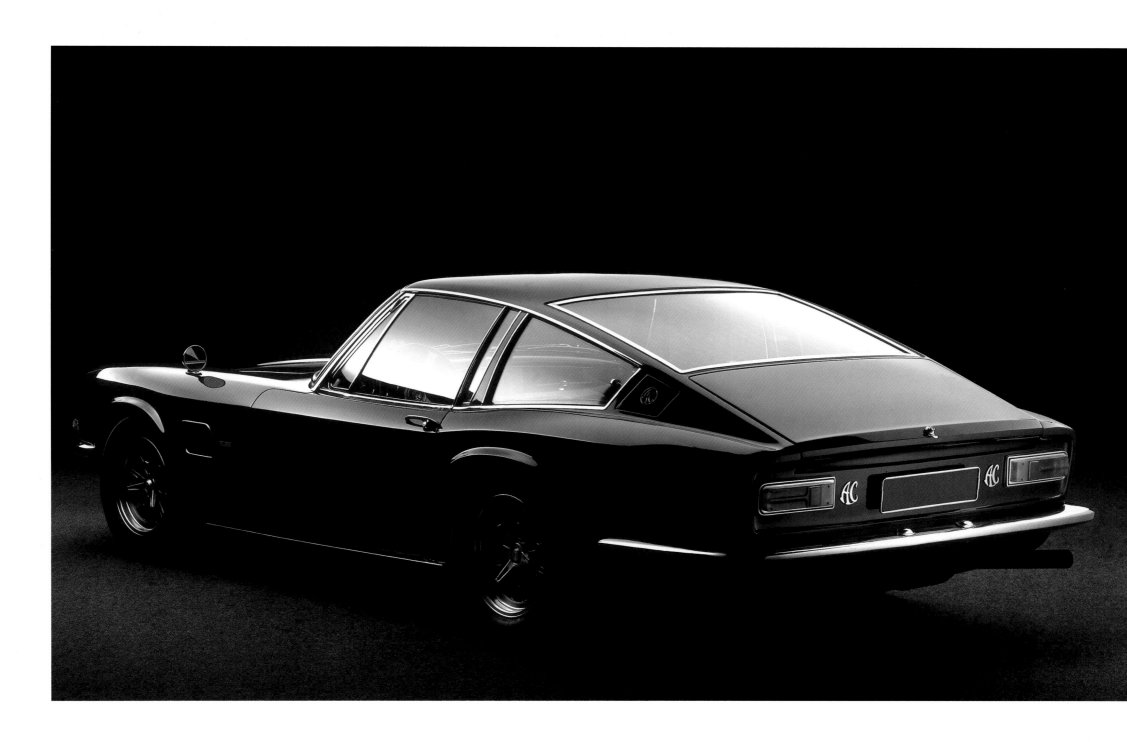

1966 JAGUAR XJ13

Jaguar has won the Le Mans 24 Hour Race seven times (the last in 1988). The XJ13 was built specifically to conquer the endurance classic, but never made it as far as France. After the Coventry firm pulled out of motor sport at the end of 1955, it was left to privateer teams to uphold the marque's honour, often with 'non-official' support from the factory. The XJ13 was essentially a tentative attempt to return to a fully fledged works effort, but today it's revered for its mesmerizing beauty – that and its estimated value of £7 million.

The XJ13 was a pet project of technical director Bill Heynes and celebrated engine designer Claude Bailey, who were keen to see the firm return to racing. Designed by aerodynamicist Malcolm Sayer, whose back catalogue included the C-type and D-type (see pp. 121 and 150), it was powered by a 502-bhp, 5-litre V12 engine. The 2748-lb (1246-kg) car was tested extensively in 1966 by Jaguar's legendary development driver, Norman Dewis. He lapped the MIRA (Motor Industry Research Association) facility near Nuneaton, Warwickshire, at a whisker over 161 mph (259 km/h), hitting 175 mph (282 km/h) on the straights and setting an unofficial lap record in the process.

Ultimately, the XJ13 was judged unlikely to prove competitive against Ford's GT40 and the Ferrari P4, so the car was mothballed, although lessons learned from developing its engine were used in Jaguar's production V12 unit, which remained a constant from 1971 to 1996. That wasn't quite the end of the story, though. After four years spent under a dustsheet, the XJ13 returned to MIRA for an appearance in a promotional film. Dewis was steering the car past the cameras at an estimated 145 mph (233 km/h) when the rear offside wheel gave way under load, flipping the car into a series of end-over-end rolls before it came to rest in the circuit's infield. Miraculously, Dewis emerged intact, and the car was restored.

Built in 1966 and first run in 1967, the XJ13 was meant to race against the Ford GT40 and Ferrari P4 at Le Mans. That never happened, not least because of a rule change that capped engine capacity at 3 litres, and the Jaguar's was 4994 cc.

The XJ13 was a racing car, so styling was low on the list of priorities; as the saying goes, everyone loves an ugly car if it wins. But with this model, Jaguar created pure kinetic sculpture in which functionality begets beauty. Little wonder that collectors are so keen to obtain the only car ever made: one offered to write a cheque for £7 million.

Designed by Malcolm Sayer, the architect behind earlier competition Jaguars, the XJ13 could conceivably have taken up the baton in the Le Mans 24 Hour Race where the D-type had left off a decade earlier. Following a crash during the making of a promotional film in 1971, the car was extensively rebuilt, with Abbey Panels re-creating the original body.

Opposite: The ultra-stark cabin displays four decades' worth of patina. Once the driver has climbed over the aluminium sill, cockpit space is tight, and a bank of gauges vies for attention. Heat builds up when the car is running: oil and water pipes run adjacent to the passenger seat.

Right: Just seven of these experimental 5-litre quad-cam V12 engines were ever made, and only two in XJ13-spec with gear-driven camshafts. A twin-cam version was later adopted for the E-type and XJ12 saloon.

1969 GILBERN INVADER

Wales has never been at the epicentre of sports-car manufacture, the Gilbern marque being its greatest export. The company was founded in 1959 by butcher Giles Smith and German-born ex-POW Bernard Friese (Gilbern being a contraction of their forenames), and the first model, the GT, was based on Austin A35 components with a choice of engines, including a race-proven Coventry Climax unit.

In 1961 a factory – actually an array of prefab sheds – was erected in Llantwit Fardre in Wales, and cars were built there at a rate of one a month. With gradual developments to the model, culminating in the MGB-powered GT1800, production had been ramped up to around one car a week by 1965. A year on, an all-new car was launched: the Genie, a much larger 2+2 coupé with Ford V6 power. Lacking the money to increase production, however, the partners sold out to the ACE group (a manufacturer of one-armed bandit slot machines, among other things) in April 1968. Smith and Friese were retained as directors, the former departing soon afterwards, and the latter assisting in developing the Genie and its replacement, the Invader.

Essentially a more sophisticated variation of the Genie, the Invader went on sale in 1969, with constant developments refining the concept. The range was augmented with an estate variant from 1971, and the company pressed ahead with a Trevor Fiore-styled, mid-engined sports car – codename T11 – that was ultimately shelved on grounds of cost. With ever-mounting debts, Gilbern changed hands several more times, lurching in and out of receivership before the end came in March 1974. Demand was still there, however, and as late as 1979 there were plans to revive the marque, but none reached fruition: building small-series sports cars has rarely been profitable. Around 1050 of all models were made.

Early Invaders were offered in component form for home assembly, but the late-model Invader Mk3 (as here) was a proper factory-made – and luxuriously equipped – sports coupé. Demand was still high when Gilbern collapsed in 1974, but the economies of scale involved in producing small-series cars were not enough for the company to continue.

1971 ROLLS-ROYCE CORNICHE

By the early 1960s Rolls-Royce Motors could no longer claim to be a leader in the field of technical excellence. Although its limousines were impeccably well made, they were outdated in appearance and wilfully antiquated of design. Arch-rival Mercedes-Benz, in particular, stole a march on the Crewe firm with its cutting-edge 600 super-saloon.

Although continuing to build stately saloons in tiny quantities, Rolls-Royce responded to foreign competition with what passed for a volume product: the Silver Shadow. The car that would become the marque's biggest-ever seller was handsomely styled by Bill Allen and could never be accused of being old-fashioned. In a major departure from earlier practices, the new model, introduced in 1965, was of monocoque construction and featured disc rather than drum brakes. Powered by a 6.2-litre (later 6.7-litre) V8 engine, the car's most striking feature was high-pressure hydraulic self-levelling suspension (licensed from Citroën), offering a bump-free ride. The Silver Shadow proved especially popular in overseas markets, with more than 38,000 being made (including Bentley-badged sister models) until 1980.

The Silver Shadow was primarily available as a saloon, but coupé and convertible editions, crafted by Mulliner Park Ward, were offered before the name of Corniche was adopted in 1971 to add extra distinction: the tag had first been applied to a 1939 Bentley prototype that didn't make it into production before war broke out. Although not intended as a performance car, the open-top model could reach 60 mph (100 km/h) from a standing start in 9.6 seconds, and 120 mph (193 km/h) overall. While the coupé was discontinued in 1982, the convertible remained in production as late as 1996, easily outliving the Silver Shadow that bore it.

Outliving the Silver Shadow that spawned it by over a decade, the Corniche was initially deemed to be gauche by Rolls-Royce traditionalists because of its modernist touches. Now it seems almost pedestrian.

JAGUAR XJ-S

Just how do you replace an icon? By the early 1970s sales of the legendary E-type were dwindling and expectations were high for its successor. Jaguar had been in the vanguard of styling excellence for nearly forty years, with the E-type (see p. 184) its pinnacle.

Reception was mixed for the XJ-S when it was introduced at the Frankfurt Motor Show in September 1975. Offered only as a coupé, this was patently more a grand tourer than a sports car. Jaguar founder Sir William Lyons was still at the helm during its conception (the XJ-S was to be the last model under his captaincy), but his design ally Malcolm Sayer had died in 1970, before the outline had been finalized, and the car's chunky buttresses, long overhangs and plastic bumpers polarized opinion.

Beyond the styling, the car's 5.3-litre V12 engine was the model of smoothness, while the all-round independent suspension proffered a supple ride. Unfortunately, by the mid-1970s Jaguar had been engulfed in the nationalized British Leyland combine, and construction quality suffered. In 1979 the model was almost dropped, but two years later saw a turnaround with the new HE (High Efficiency) edition, which featured various detail improvements, including a new cylinder-head design. A 3.6-litre six-cylinder engine was added to the line-up in 1983 with the arrival of the new cabriolet model, which was replaced by a full convertible in 1988. On the race track, Tom Walkinshaw won the 1984 European Touring Car Championship drivers' title in an XJ-S, his TWR team's expertise culminating with the factory-sponsored 318-bhp 6-litre XJR-S edition four years later. Sales were booming and, following Ford's takeover in 1990, a raft of engineering tweaks resulted in a new strain of XJS (minus the hyphen) that maintained the model's relevance until it was finally killed off in April 1996.

Once thought of as a poor replacement for the beloved E-type, the XJ-S has undergone a critical re-evaluation of late. Launched when Jaguar was mired in British Leyland control, it excelled when the marque gained its independence and maintained its importance under later Ford custodianship.

The removal of the roof to create a convertible Jaguar XJ-S was a masterstroke and did away with the awkward rear buttresses of the coupé. The idea of an open variation was initially mooted by coachbuilder Lynx, which created its first Spider in 1980, easily pre-dating the factory offering.

Large tail light clusters, chunky plastic bumpers and a long rear overhang were three styling features that were initially criticized; more than thirty years later, they don't seem remotely controversial.

1976 LOTUS ESPRIT

Perhaps the most enduring supercar of them all, the Esprit grew out of a concept dubbed the 'silver car', shown at the Turin Motor Show in November 1972. Styled by Giorgetto Giugiaro, and based on a Lotus Europa chassis, it prompted marque-founder Colin Chapman to adopt it as a production model. The first definitive Esprit prototype was shown at the following year's Geneva Salon, although customers had to wait until 1976 before receiving their cars.

Initially plagued with reliability issues, the Esprit matured into a rewarding drivers' car; one that would routinely go under the knife for cosmetic and technical changes to sustain its place in the supercar firmament.

Based on a pressed-steel backbone chassis, and powered by a mid-mounted 1973-cc twin-cam 16-valve four-cylinder engine, this wedge-shaped car initially suffered from excessive vibrations and cooling problems. Just 714 of the Series 1 cars were made before the revised S2, which addressed at least some of the problems, was launched in 1978.

In 1980 Lotus ushered in a turbocharged variant with revised bodywork, again styled by Giugiaro. With engine capacity enlarged to 2.2 litres, and producing 210 bhp, it finally had enough power to back up its dramatic looks. Despite the relatively small engine, the glassfibre-bodied projectile could reach 60 mph (100 km/h) in 6.1 seconds, and had a maximum speed of 148 mph (238 km/h).

In 1987 the Esprit gained another substantial makeover when in-house designer Peter Stevens masterfully softened the edges of the by-then very dated 'folded paper' outline. Later styling revisions by Julian Thompson and Russell Carr continued to maintain the car's relevance, the ultimate iteration being the V8, released in 1996. Powered by Lotus's Type 918, 3.5-litre twin-turbocharged unit, it could comfortably top 160 mph (257 km/h) and reach 0–60 mph (100 km/h) in under 5 seconds. Esprit production continued to tick over until 2004, and over a twenty-eight-year period, a total of 10,675 Esprits were produced. Lotus periodically talks about reviving the name, although manufacture of any new car could be farmed out to Malaysia.

In 1980 the Esprit received the first of its many makeovers, original stylist Giorgetto Giugiaro adding new spoilers and other glassfibre additions, along with Rover SD1 rear light clusters.

In turbocharged 2.2-litre trim, the Esprit belied its meagre engine capacity with blistering performance. The subsequent arrival of a 3.5-litre V8 edition ensured that it took the fight to Ferrari and other Italian exotica.

1978 JAGUAR XJ SPIDER
PININFARINA

It was a teaser, a one-off intended to impress a major manufacturer as much as Everyman. In the late 1970s Italian design studio Pininfarina was contracted by Jaguar to carry out a facelift on its XJ6/12; the end product was subtle and beautifully realized, and went on sale in 1979. The Spider wasn't built at Jaguar's behest, but Pininfarina took a flyer anyway: the car could conceivably have been adopted by the marque as a production model, but more likely it would lead to more design work – if it impressed.

And it did. Despite the project's unofficial status, Jaguar went as far as to donate an XJ-S development hack, which was shipped over to Turin where it was filleted until all that remained was the bare floorpan. Under the direction of Pininfarina's head of research and development, Lorenzo Ramaciotti, the new body was formed from metal and aluminium and then honed in a wind tunnel. Styling cues were drawn from Jaguar's back catalogue, with hints of both D- and E-types (see pp. 150 and 184) to its long snout, swoopy beltline and ovoid front air-intake. Outwardly, it appeared to be both cutting-edge and traditional without being clichéd. Inside, Pininfarina eschewed the usual Jaguar 'trees and cows' approach. There was leather, but it was rolled around the door cards and seat edges, and there was no wood: a blank Perspex screen in the dashboard concealed a digital read-out display, and minor controls were grouped together in the centre console.

Unveiled at the 1978 British Motor Show in Birmingham, the dark-green XJ Spider captivated everyone, the only controversial note being the high tail, which today doesn't appear at all radical. It's easy to speculate that, had it gone into production, the Spider would have been a roaring success. But it didn't. And the next time Pininfarina was let near a Jaguar was in the mid-1990s, when it customized a batch of XJ220s (see p. 259) for the Sultan of Brunei.

One of the great 'what if?' stories in Jaguar lore, this Italianate take on the classic British roadster could have – should have – been a contender. Its achingly pretty styling still appears contemporary.

In profile, the Spider echoes styling themes explored earlier on the E-type. Built as a teaser (a show car), it nonetheless hinted at the likelihood of production. Sadly, it ultimately remained unique.

Opposite: The XJ Spider Pininfarina's hind treatment, with its cropped tail and distinctive lighting arrangement, was considered to be highly controversial at the time. Now it's hard to see what all the fuss was about.

Right: A very Italian Jaguar, the XJ Spider did away with the traditional walnut dashboard; in its place was a heavily sculptured, leather-clad affair with a Perspex screen, behind which were mounted electronic instruments. This was cutting edge at the time, and is the only area in which the car has dated.

ASTON MARTIN V8 ZAGATO

The deposits flooded in on the basis of a single styling sketch. For £15,000 you too could add your name to the waiting list – if you were quick enough and had the remaining £55,000 – to own one of these intriguing Anglo-Italian super-coupés. The price tag is a lot of money today; it was even more in 1985, but the entire limited run of fifty cars was sold before the first had even been built.

The car's gestation period was a brief one. The marriage of Aston Martin's beefy engineering and Zagato's styling flair had resulted in a superlative competition-orientated coupé two decades earlier (see p. 177). A visit from Elio and Gianni Zagato to Aston Martin's stand at the 1984 Geneva Salon sparked an attempt to bottle lightning a second time. Aston Martin chairman Victor Gauntlett was keen to re-ignite interest in the marque, as sales of the existing V8 Vantage were ebbing and flowing as the company papered over the cracks of an ageing model line-up. Reworking the long-serving platform with a new body – and then charging a massive premium – would help fund the proposed Project DP1999 'baby' Aston. Shortly after the Geneva meeting, the go-ahead was given.

By the time the prototype broke cover at the 1986 Geneva Salon, it was substantially different from the rendering of two years before. Some 16 in. (406 mm) shorter than the Vantage donor, it appeared stubby and purposeful, but by shedding flab – it was 10 per cent lighter than the existing model – and creating a more aerodynamic profile, the 435-bhp V8 Zagato could reach 186 mph (300 km/h) and 60 mph (100 km/h) from standstill in 4.8 seconds. By the time the last of the fifty-two cars had been completed, in 1988, the list price had risen to an eye-watering £145,000. Predictably keen to repeat the formula, Aston Martin ushered in an open-top Volante edition in the same year, taking thirty-seven deposits for the planned run of twenty-five cars. Inevitably, Aston Martin built thirty-seven.

It was unconventionally attractive to some, conventionally unattractive to others; one thing most are agreed on is that Zagato's riff on the Aston Martin V8 theme was more aerodynamic and lighter than the car upon which it was based.

Opposite: The V8 Zagato's cabin architecture was a mix of traditional Aston Martin and idiosyncratic Italian design. The cubist dashboard wasn't altogether attractive, but expansive side glazing afforded panoramic all-round visibility.

Below: The end result looked substantially different to the original rendering. Even so, the entire production run was sold long before the first car reached its expectant owner. If anything, the subsequent convertible variant was better looking.

1988 JAGUAR XJ220

By the end of the 1980s, it seemed as though not a week went by without a new supercar being launched. Most disappeared into the ether before the ink on the press release was dry, but the XJ220 almost made the grade. Almost. That it's latterly been viewed as a flop is largely due to the effect of outside forces on its progress, although wholesale changes made between the concept car and the resultant production version didn't help.

The XJ220 grew out of a secret project initiated by Jaguar employees who gathered after hours as the 'Saturday Club'. The firm's chief engineer, Jim Randle, envisaged a contemporary version of the stillborn XJ13 (see p. 227), one capable of bettering 200 mph (322 km/h). Jaguar's management was impressed by the concept and committed the firm to producing a car in time for the 1988 British Motor Show. The company's motor-sport partner, Tom Walkinshaw Racing (TWR), would produce a 6.2-litre version of Jaguar's legendary V12, while FF Developments would engineer the four-wheel-drive system.

The original show car was a huge hit, with the Keith Helfet-styled outline proving more than a match for Latin exotica. When it was announced as a production model in 1989, with a launch price of a heady £361,000, speculators were tripping over themselves to hand over deposits totalling £50,000. Jaguar promised that just 350 cars would be made.

By the time the definitive XJ220 went into production in late 1991, it differed greatly from the original concept. The scissor doors had been replaced by more conventional ones, while under the bonnet the V12 had made way for a twin-turbocharged V6. The four-wheel-drive arrangement had been ditched for rear-wheel drive only. With a downturn in the global economy, many potential customers cited the changes as grounds for legal action to reclaim deposits. The fact that the XJ220 was – and remains – an impressive performance car capable of 217 mph (350 km/h) meant little. The plug was pulled after 281 cars had been made.

The XJ220 was an unsung supercar. A change of specification from prototype to production car, allied to a collapse in the global economy, conspired to sully its reputation as a performance icon. Even so, it was once the fastest road car on sale anywhere.

Despite being built with speeds of
more than 200 mph (340 km/h) in
mind, the XJ220 nonetheless confirmed
Jaguar's reputation for comfort and
civility. Although the car's low roofline
makes it a pain to get into, once
one is seated it's surprisingly palatial
for a supercar.

If ever a supercar could be described as sculpture, this one would be. The XJ220 was a styling masterclass, even if its vast size intimidated some and infuriated others.

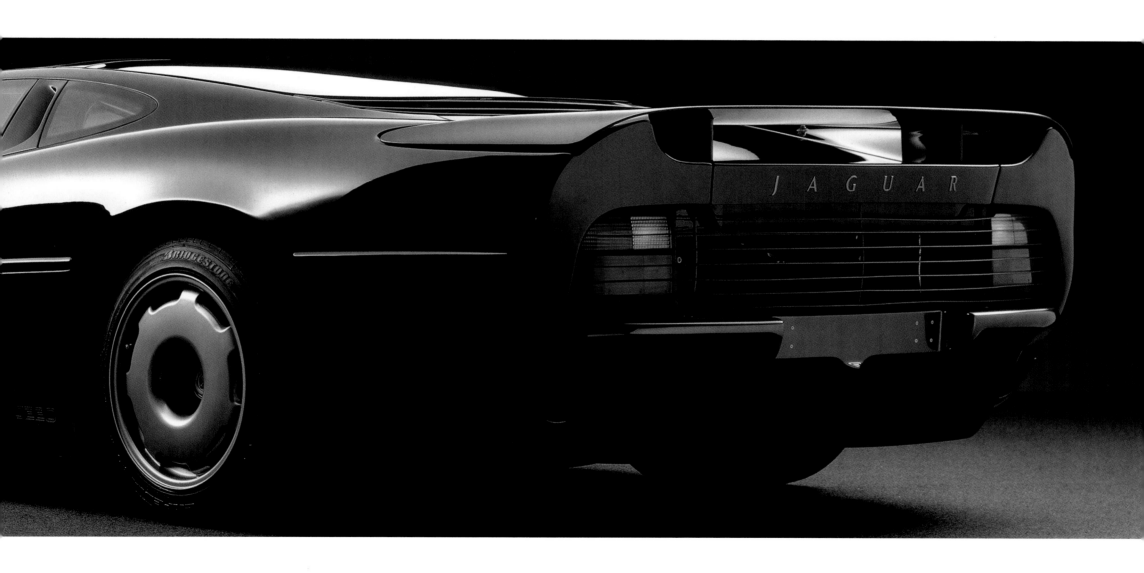

Styled by the South African Keith Helfet, the XJ220 eschewed quick-to-date additions, displaying instead a purity of line lacking on most of its rivals. The oval front grille is a nod to such earlier Jaguar legends as the D- and E-types.

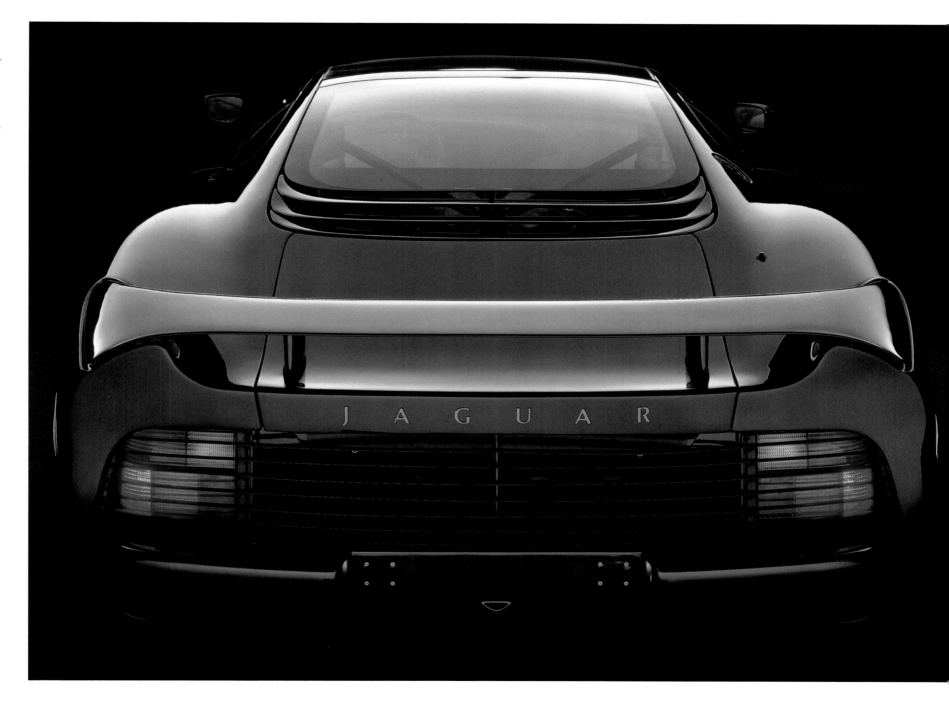

ASTON MARTIN DB7

In 1991 Aston Martin made just forty-six cars. Between September 1994 and December 2003, it made around 7000 DB7s. The importance of this car to the very survival of this calamity-prone marque cannot be overestimated. Its unveiling at the Geneva Salon in March 1993 marked the dawn of a new breed of Astons, with old-school craftsmanship making way for mass-production techniques. Some bemoaned the DB7's largely composite method of body construction, which Aston Martin favoured over the time-honoured hand-beaten aluminium approach. Others sniffed at its Jaguar heritage. But even the doubters couldn't argue with its success.

Much of this was down to the DB7's styling. Ian Callum's masterful handiwork was offered in coupé or convertible Volante (from 1996) configurations, each elegant and redolent of past Astons but without veering towards retro pastiche. The DB7, known internally as Project NPX, marked the first Aston designed entirely under the Ford Motor Company's tenure, the Detroit giant having acquired the British minnow in 1988. It was also the first to be built at a factory in Bloxham, Oxfordshire (previously used for the construction of Jaguar's XJ220), rather than at the firm's spiritual home of Newport Pagnell, Buckinghamshire.

The DB7's platform was effectively an evolution of the by-then aged Jaguar XJ-S (see p. 238), its super-charged 3239-cc straight-six engine being developed by technical partner TWR from an existing Jaguar unit. And if 335 bhp wasn't enough, the works' service department offered a special 'Driving Dynamics' package, which enhanced performance and handling for those wanting something a little more dramatic.

In 1999 an altogether more brutish variation was introduced. Callum's styling makeover for the Vantage edition featured revised grilles, sills and lights, along with a more muscular hind treatment. Beneath the skin, it featured a new all-aluminium, 48-valve V12 engine developed in conjunction with Cosworth Technology that produced 400 bhp, enough power to propel the car to 184 mph (296 km/h) and 0–60 mph (100 km/h) in 5 seconds. By the time the model ceased production, 4458 examples had been made, the last six-cylinder car being completed in May 1999.

Arguably the most beautiful production car of the 1990s, the DB7 revitalized Aston Martin and undoubtedly saved the marque from oblivion. While some traditionalists hated that it wasn't handcrafted, the model helped establish the calamity-prone marque as a volume manufacturer.

Below: All the DB7's design work was done by outside firm TWR (Tom Walkinshaw Racing); its stylist, Ian Callum, filled his studio with pictures of the classic DB5 to act as a reference point.

Opposite: Although attractive, the DB7's cabin was never entirely successful, as there was precious little headroom and rear visibility was virtually non-existent. Minor controls stolen from the Ford parts bin also cheapened the mood.

1996   JAGUAR XK8

Unveiled at the Geneva Salon in March 1996, the XK8 swiftly became one of the bestselling Jaguars of all time, replacing the long-serving XJ-S (see p. 238), from which it borrowed its basic architecture. The car's styling was the work of Geoff Lawson and Keith Helfet, and evoked memories of the hallowed E-type, even if the rear overhang rendered it a mite flabby. (Rumour has it that the rump was shaped so that the boot could house two fully stocked golf bags.) Some criticized the XK8's likeness to the Aston Martin DB7 (see p. 264) – another Ford-owned brand – although the Jaguar was actually designed first.

The XK8 officially went on sale in October 1996, with a launch price of £47,950 in coupé form, and £56,850 in convertible configuration. It was powered by the all-new, all-aluminium, 290-bhp AJ-V8 engine driving through a five-speed automatic transmission, and its top speed was electronically restricted to 155 mph (250 km/h). A 370-bhp supercharged variant, the XKR, followed in May 1998. To tie in with the arrival of Jaguar's Formula One team (which proved a folly of epic proportions), a limited run of 100 'Silverstone' XKRs (half of them coupés, the rest convertibles) was offered in April 2000, all finished in a striking shade of platinum. Countless special editions followed on the home and North American markets, including the XK Victory, which trumpeted the marque's success in the Trans-Am racing series. The XK8 also found some measure of fame on the silver screen, making appearances in the spy-spoof *Austin Powers: Goldmember* and the James Bond film *Die Another Day*.

The last XK8 rolled off the production line in Browns Lane, Coventry, on 24 May 2005, by which time 91,406 cars had been made. Although the car has yet to achieve classic status, its role as a standard-bearer during Jaguar's often rollercoaster existence under Ford's stewardship is assured.

Perhaps not the hoped-for spiritual successor to the E-type, the XK8 nevertheless represented a quantum leap forward stylistically over the outgoing XJ-S. Although it was forever in the shadow of its half-sister, the Aston Martin DB7, the XK8 was in many ways the better car.

1998 JAGUAR XK180

Time was when Jaguar's design language was predictive rather than reactionary, the E-type being a prime example (see p. 184). Somewhere along the way, all of that was forgotten as the marque became mired in ultra-conservatism and, conversely, copyist retro-faddism. When unveiled at the 1998 Paris Motor Show, the XK180 concept car did at least remind onlookers that the Coventry firm was still capable of creating an object of beauty.

Although the XK180 was never intended as a production car, the alluring design study was fully functional. Styled by Keith Helfet, whose back catalogue included the XJ220 (see p. 259), the prototype was handmade in Jaguar's special vehicle operations department. A production XKR (supercharged version of the XK8, see p. 269) donor car was disassembled, its chassis shortened by 5 in. (127 mm), before it was reclothed with a new aluminium bodyshell formed at Abbey Panels in Coventry. Mechanically it was pure XKR, although its V8 engine was tuned to produce 450 bhp. A five-speed automatic transmission incorporated a selector system made in-house that enabled gear changes to be made using push-buttons located on the steering wheel. Created to celebrate the fiftieth anniversary of the legendary XK120 (see p. 111), the XK180 was given a numerical designation that signified its top speed in miles per hour (like the designation of the XK120), although no independent figures verified the performance claims.

A second example, this time in left-hand-drive configuration, was unveiled at the 1999 Detroit Motor Show. It was, if anything, sexier still, with subtle alterations to the lower body sections and new 20-in. (508-mm) wheels. Sadly, however, the XK180 was to remain just a tease, although it was probably the most attractive concept car of the decade. Considering the opposition, that's some accolade.

Styling studies all too often hint at the future without giving much thought to the present. The XK180 was more a case of taking a product that was still relatively new — the XK8 — and radicalizing it. The result was breathtaking.

Below: As with the XJ220, the XK180's styling was the work of Keith Helfet. The bodywork for both prototypes was crafted by Abbey Panels, the same firm that decades earlier had created the XJ13's aluminium skin.

Opposite: It wasn't very practical to use so much leather in a car with no roof, even of the temporary variety — but then, this was a show car. The machine-tuned aluminium dashboard is as old an automotive design treatment as the motor car itself.

Possibly the sexiest concept car of the 1990s, the XK180 was just a tease: Jaguar had no intention of ever putting it into production. Considering some of the models that followed, this was a pity.

THE NAMES BEHIND
THE LEGENDS

HERBERT AUSTIN
1866–1941

Inextricably linked to two famous names, Wolseley and his own eponymous marque, Herbert Austin had a great gift for making cars that were affordable for Everyman. His company's slogan was: 'You buy a car but you invest in an Austin.' And, for several decades, seemingly *everyone* bought an Austin.

This farmer's son emigrated to Australia in 1884 and found work with the Wolseley Sheep Shearing Machine Co., run by fellow Englishman Frederick Wolseley. He made many improvements to Wolseley's machines and, in October 1889, the duo moved back to England and set up shop in Birmingham. Austin devised his first car in 1895 along the lines of Léon Bollée's 'Voiturette', but the definitive production Wolseley Autocar No. 1 went on sale a year later. Striking out on his own in December 1905, Austin had his greatest success with the Austin Seven (see p. 39), and by 1934 the Austin Motor Co. was Britain's largest car manufacturer. Knighted in 1917 for his war efforts, Austin was a Tory MP from 1918 to 1925 and was made Baron Austin of Longbridge in 1936; apparently, this title didn't sit well with the unpretentious engineer.

WALTER OWEN BENTLEY
1888–1971

Like his great rival Henry Royce, 'W.O.' Bentley began his career as a railway engineering apprentice. Having hitherto been dismissive of the automobile, he bought his first — a Riley V-twin — in 1910, shortly before taking a job with the National Motor Cab Co., which owned a concession for the French DFP marque. Bentley refined the design and won races at the Brooklands circuit in Surrey before seeing duty with the Royal Naval Service during World War II.

Bentley the marque, announced in 1919 before a prototype even existed, was slow in gestation, with the first car not being delivered until 1921. Although hugely successful in motor racing, Bentley Motors was always short of cash and, despite a virtual takeover by backer Woolf Barnato in 1925, the firm was swallowed up by Rolls-Royce six years later. W.O., as he was always known, subsequently designed engines for Lagonda — one of which was adopted for the Aston Martin DB2, and another for an Armstrong-Siddeley that didn't enter production — before he retired to bask in the warm glow of appreciation from members of the Bentley Drivers' Club.

SIR DAVID BROWN
1904–1993

During Aston Martin's often calamity-prone existence, its longest period of stability as an independent marque was arguably under the tenure of this hard-to-please Yorkshireman. David Brown was born into engineering stock, and conceived a 1.5-litre, straight-eight engine while still an apprentice in the family gear-manufacturing business. That first engine was never finished, but Brown had constructed a one-off Meadows-powered sports car called the Davbro by the time he assumed control of the family business in 1932, and made an even bigger splash making tractors.

After World War II, Brown had the means to indulge himself. He bought Aston Martin for £25,000 in February 1947 and scooped Lagonda for £52,500 a few months later. He would return both brands to prosperity, the former claiming several honours in motor sport during the 1950s. Brown relished his role as a motor mogul and enjoyed the prestige of having his initials attached to the luxury Aston DB series, even if there was little profit in it. He was knighted in 1968, and divested himself of Aston Martin Lagonda in 1972.

COLIN CHAPMAN
1928–1982

Lotus founder Anthony Colin Bruce Chapman was a colossus of motor sport, a wayward genius renowned for breaking moulds and pushing boundaries. His real ability was in harnessing (some might say exploiting) the talents of others, enlisting a roll-call of legendary designers and engineers all too willing to work impossible hours just to follow in their employer's wake.

After he had been turned down for pilot training in the RAF, Chapman discovered cars and began work on his first Lotus in 1947. Within twenty years the marque had won the Formula One drivers' and constructors' championships and the Indianapolis 500. It also fashioned such landmark road cars as the Elite, the Elan and the Ford Lotus-Cortina.

Ultimately, Chapman's reputation would be besmirched by his contribution to the DeLorean scandal: Lotus was responsible for turning the DeLorean DMC12 – an American-devised sports car sponsored by the British government – into a production reality. When millions of taxpayers' pounds ended up in Swiss bank accounts a storm erupted, but Chapman died of a heart attack before facing a likely prison sentence.

CECIL KIMBER
1888–1945

Cecil Kimber, widely regarded as the father of the MG marque, owed his life's creation to a small link with a failed business venture. He invested – and lost – most of his modest savings in E.G. Wriggley, a component manufacturer that supplied, among others, Morris Cars. Then in 1921 he became sales manager of Morris Garages in Oxford. There he built a one-off special based on a Morris Cowley chassis: the MG was born. The MG Car Co. came into being in January 1928, with Kimber being made managing director two years later. He was a keen supporter of motor sport, and the factory-backed team found huge success and raked in publicity until MG was taken over by Morris Motors in 1935. Morris's hard-headed principal, Leonard Lord, was hostile to what he perceived as a waste of money.

Kimber was then effectively dismissed in 1941; he had secured a contract to make the frontal section of the Albemarle bomber in a bid to keep the factory up and running, but he hadn't consulted his paymasters first. He subsequently found employment with coachbuilders Charlesworth. Kimber died in a freak railway accident at King's Cross Station.

SIR WILLIAM LYONS
1901–1985

Although the founder of Jaguar Cars was primarily a hard-nosed businessman, his greatest gift was his innate sense of style. Bill Lyons was not a great draughtsman or model-maker, but – like many Italian coachbuilders – he worked best by eye. He would toil outdoors with a favoured panel beater and direct the shaping of a prototype's body. Lyons was rarely original, but his magpie approach invariably resulted in him improving on whatever provided inspiration: witness the XK120 (see p. 111) borrowing its basic outline from the BMW 328MM.

Born and raised in Blackpool, Lancashire, Lyons found some measure of early fame making sidecars under the Swallow moniker before clothing proprietary automobile chassis. This in turn led to the SS marque and then Jaguar, with Lyons creating fast, capable and often exquisite machines at knockdown prices; only his penny-pinching ultimately sold his cars short. He merged Jaguar with the British Motor Corporation in 1966 and remained chairman of Jaguars Cars until his retirement in 1972. Lyons was knighted in 1956.

LIONEL MARTIN
1878–1945

Although largely forgotten in British motoring history, this Old Etonian was responsible for creating the Aston Martin marque. Born into wealth (his family owned china clay mines in Cornwall), Martin was a keen bicyclist for most of his life, and competed on two wheels with some success. Shortly before the outbreak of World War I, he began his modest motor-sport career, campaigning a Singer Ten to class honours at the Aston Clinton hillclimb course in 1913. That same year he entered into partnership with Robert Bamford and built a special that comprised an Isotta-Fraschini chassis and 1389-cc Coventry-Simplex engine. Needing an appellation for the beast, he combined the name of the scene of his racing triumph and his surname: Aston Martin.

The marque officially arrived in 1921, but its life with its creator was short. Having spent upwards of £150,000 – in addition to outside finance – trying to make a go of the automobile business, Martin called it quits in November 1925 and subsequently concentrated on mining interests. He died after being knocked off his tricycle in Kingston upon Thames, Surrey.

CHARLES STEWART ROLLS
1877–1910

Reputedly a cold and solitary man, Charles Rolls was the son of Lord and Lady Llangattock of Monmouthshire. While studying engineering at Trinity College, Cambridge, he bought a 3½-hp Peugeot, which – in 1896 – was probably the first car ever to be seen within this city of learning. Three years later he discovered motor sport, driving a Panhard to fifth overall in the Paris–Boulogne race.

Being sufficiently wealthy that he never needed to earn a living, Rolls nevertheless built up his interest in cars into a reasonably lucrative business as a Mors and Panhard agent. Being the patriotic sort, he was disappointed by the lack of credible British automobiles until he was introduced to Henry Royce. Rolls was impressed enough by the near-silent running of the Royce motor car to take the entire output, but on the condition that bigger-engined cars be made and that all future models should be labelled Rolls-Royce. However, Rolls soon became bored with cars and turned his attention to the skies; he died after crashing his biplane during a flying display at Bournemouth.

SIR HENRY ROYCE
1863–1933

A great engineer but a reluctant knight, Henry Royce was diametrically opposed in background and outlook to Charles Rolls, with whom his name would become forever linked. He was born in Lincolnshire, but his miller father moved the family to London when Henry was just four. By the time Royce entered his teens, he'd already been working for three years in a variety of menial jobs, and it was an aunt who set him on the path to success by helping fund an apprenticeship with the Great Northern Railway.

After Royce had joined forces with his friend Ernest Claremont in 1884, the two men devised and patented various machines, including an electric crane, before the first Royce car left their workshop in Clarke Street, Manchester, on 1 April 1904. Royce was a workaholic who often forgot to eat, and his health suffered. Having fallen gravely ill in 1911, he was given months to live but confounded all by surviving a further twenty-two years. He remained involved in numerous automotive and aeronautical projects for the rest of his life, working through intermediaries from his homes in Sussex and Le Canadel, France. He was made a baronet in 1931.

MALCOLM SAYER
1916–1970

A modest yet hugely talented man, Malcolm Sayer contributed greatly to Jaguar's role as a style leader in the two decades following World War II. That he also helped establish the Coventry marque as a major player in motor sport during the 1950s should have long since ensured his place in automotive history, but he was always content working in the shadow of his boss and collaborator, Sir William Lyons.

After graduating from Loughborough College, Leicestershire, with first-class honours in automotive engineering, Sayer joined the Bristol Aerospace Company, where he applied his understanding of aerodynamics to several World War II aircraft. In 1948 he moved to Iraq to take up a post at the University of Baghdad but discovered that the job existed only on paper. Two years later he joined Jaguar Cars and played a major role in designing the C-type that won at Le Mans first time out in 1951, followed by the D-type and legendary E-type (see pp. 150 and 184). He remained with the firm until his death at the age of just fifty-four.

GLOSSARY OF MOTORING TERMS AND STYLES

Axle
Shaft carrying the wheels and supporting the body via the road springs. Also refers to non-shaft wheel pairings transversely across the car in independent suspension.

Beam axle
Rigid shaft (not independently sprung) carrying and linking front wheels.

Cam
Eccentric projection, usually elliptical in shape, on a shaft; it moves another component as the shaft revolves.

Camshaft
Shaft that revolves within a housing, often incorporating a number of cams, usually to operate valve gear. Can be driven by gears, chains or belts.

Carburettor
Mechanism that mixes petrol with air to atomize it and delivers this mixture to the engine inlet valves.

It automatically adjusts mixture to suit the engine, road speed and atmospheric conditions.

Coil springs
Suspension mechanism of sprung-steel wire coiled into a helix.

Cubic capacity
Measurement of the total volume of an engine's cylinders swept by each piston in its bore. Engine capacity is measured in cubic centimetres (cc) or litres, 1000 cc being 1 litre; or in cubic inches, 1 cu. in. being 16.39 cc.

Gullwing
Doors that are hinged in the roof to open upwards.

Independent suspension
Method of attaching a vehicle's wheels so that each has its own independent linkage to the chassis or body. Each wheel is sprung independently so that it can move without affecting any other.

Ladderframe chassis
Chassis in which two spars are laid longitudinally and connected transversely by strengthening and support webs.

Leaf springs
Flat tempered steel joined together to form an elliptical shape in order to provide a springing effect between the axles and the car's chassis or body.

Live rear axle
Transverse beam axle connecting both road wheels and housing the differential and final drive.

Monoblock
Engine construction in which crankcase and cylinder block are cast in one piece.

Monocoque
Single-skin car body lacking longitudinal members.

Overhead camshaft
Camshaft(s) mounted above the cylinder head, at the opposite end from the crankshaft.

Overhead valve
An arrangement of the camshaft in the engine block whereby the valve gear is operated by pushrods situated above the cylinder head.

Panhard rod
An axle's lateral location device, situated between the car's body or chassis on one side, and an axle on the other.

Piston
A cylindrical component with one end closed and the other open, sealed into the engine cylinder with piston rings. Driven down the cylinder bore by the exploding fuel mixture, it bears on the connecting rods, which force the crankshaft to twist.

rpm
Revolution per minute. Any measure of rotational speed. Usually refers to a crankshaft but can also refer to road wheels.

Running gear
Components that underpin a car, especially engine, suspension and axles.

Scuttle
A bulkhead, often between the car's front occupants and the engine.

Semi-elliptic springs
A flat sprung-steel plate, or plates riveted together, forming a semi-ellipse in which the ends are joined to the body or chassis and the centre is joined to the axle. Semi-elliptical springs can be used in pairs as part of a live axle installation, or to create an independent suspension by fastening the spring transversely across the car, attaching it to the chassis in the centre and to the suspension at either end. In elliptical springs, one part is joined to the body and one to the axle. Quarter elliptics are only a quarter of an ellipse.

Sidevalve engine
Engine block in which inlet exhaust valves are arranged alongside cylinders. Huge volumetric inefficiencies are inherent in this design, so manufacturers produced more efficient, better-breathing overhead-valve and then overhead-cam engines.

Spaceframe
A lightweight rigid framework made from chassis tubes in a geometric pattern to carry all the car's systems and provide a structure on which to hang the bodywork.

Straight-six
Term that describes an engine in which six cylinders are arranged in a straight line. Cylinders may also be arranged in a 'straight-eight' or other even-number configurations.

Supercharger
Mechanical air compressor used to charge an engine's cylinders with a greater quantity of petrol-and-air mixture than that inducted naturally.

Superleggera
Italian term for a spaceframe, meaning 'super-light'.

Torsion bar
A sprung-steel bar used as a suspension mechanism in some applications by fastening the bar at one end and connecting it to a lever at the other.

Transaxle
A combined gearbox and final-drive unit positioned at the centreline of a drive axle and used to improve the car's balance or to save space through its compactness.

Turbocharger
A supercharger powered by the energy in the exhaust gases to compress the inlet charge.

Twin-cam
Term that describes the positioning of more than one camshaft, usually in a cylinder head, so that each camshaft operates directly above the valves it opens. This arrangement allows the engine designer to place the valves in the cylinder head at an optimal angle for the best gas flow, so increasing the engine's volumetric efficiency.

Wheelbase
Distance between the longitudinal centrelines of a vehicle's axles.

Wishbone
Pivoted, triangular links that connect a car's body or chassis to each wheel to form an independent suspension system.

DIRECTORY OF MUSEUMS AND COLLECTIONS

FRANCE

The Schlumpf Collection/National
Motor Museum
192 avenue de Colmar
68051 Mulhouse
Tel: +33 (0)3 89 33 23 23
collection-schlumpf.com

GERMANY

Motortechnica
Weserstrasse 225
32547 Bad Oeynhausen
Tel: +49 (0)573 19966
oldtimer.de/Museen/Oeynhausen/
Motortechnica.htm

MALTA

Malta Classic Car Collection
Tourists Street
Qawra SPB05
Tel: +356 (0)2157 8885
classiccarsmalta.com

MONACO

Collection de voitures anciennes du
SAS le Prince de Monaco
Les Terrasses de Fontvielle
MC 98000 Monaco
Tel: +377 (0)92 05 28 56
mtcc.mc

THE NETHERLANDS

Het Amsterdams Automuseum
Zwanenburgerdijk 281
1161 NL Zwanenburg
Tel: +31 (0)20 497 72 91
amsterdams-automuseum.nl

SWITZERLAND

Collection 'Gaston'
Fondation E. et C.R.
Chemin des Graviers 5
CH-2016 Cortaillod/NE
Tel: +41 (0)32 842 15 65

UNITED KINGDOM

The Atwell-Wilson Motor
Museum Trust
Downside
Stockley Lane
Calne
Wiltshire SN11 0NF
Tel: +44 (0)1249 813119
atwellwilson.org.uk

Brooklands Museum
Brooklands Road
West Byfleet
Weybridge
Surrey KT13 0QN
Tel: +44 (0)1932 857381
brooklandsmuseum.com

Cotswold Motoring Museum
& Toy Collection
The Old Mill
Burton-on-the-Water
Cheltenham
Gloucestershire GL54 2BY
Tel: +44 (0)1451 821255
cotswold-motor-museum.co.uk

Glasgow Museum of Transport
Kelvin Hall
1 Bunhouse Road
Glasgow G3 8DP
Tel: +44 (0)141 287 2720
glasgowmuseum.com

Haynes International Motor Museum
Sparkford
Yeovil
Somerset BA22 7LH
Tel: +44 (0)1963 440804
haynesmotormuseum.com

Heritage Motor Centre
Banbury Road
Gaydon
Warwickshire CV35 0BJ
Tel: +44 (0)1926 641188
heritage-motor-centre.co.uk

Jaguar Daimler Heritage Trust
Browns Lane
Allesley
Coventry CV5 9DR
Tel: +44 (0)2476 203222
jdht.com

Kew Transport Museum
110 North Road
Kew
Richmond
Surrey TW9 3QA
Tel: contact via website
ktm.itgo.com

Moray Motor Museum
Bridge Street
Elgin
Grampian IV30 2DE
Tel: +44 (0)1343 544933

Mouldsworth Motor Museum
Smithy Lane
Mouldsworth
Cheshire CH3 8AR
Tel: contact via website
mouldsworthmotormuseum.com

National Motor Museum
John Montagu Building
Beaulieu
Brockenhurst
Hampshire SO42 7ZN
Tel: +44 (0)1590 612345
beaulieu.co.uk

Pembrokeshire Motor Museum
Keeston Hill
Near Haverfordwest
Pembrokeshire SA62 6EJ
Tel: +44 (0)1437 710950
pembsmotormuseum.co.uk

Stondon Transport Museum
Station Road
Lower Stondon
Henlow
Bedfordshire SG16 6JN
Tel: +44 (0)1462 856339
transportmuseum.co.uk

UNITED STATES

Blackhawk Automotive Museum
3700 Blackhawk Plaza Circle
Damville, CA 94506
Tel: +1 925 736 2277
blackhawkauto.org

Lane Motor Museum
702 Murfreesboro Pike
Nashville, TN 37210
Tel: +1 615 742 7445
lanemotormuseum.org

INDEX